FOR

PATRIOTIC TYPES

& Others Who Want to Serve Their Country

VGM Careers for You Series

CAREERS FOR
PATRIOTIC TYPES
& Others Who Want to Serve Their Country

Jan Goldberg

VGM Career Horizons
NTC/Contemporary Publishing Group

Library of Congress Cataloging-in-Publication Data

Goldberg, Jan.
    Careers for patriotic types & others who want to serve their
country / Jan Goldberg.
        p.   cm. — (VGM careers for you series)
    ISBN 0-8442-2959-8 (cloth). — ISBN 0-8442-2960-1 (pbk.)
    1. Vocational guidance—United States.   I. Title.   II. Title:
Careers for patriotic types and others who want to serve their
country.   III. Series: VGM careers for you series.
HF5382.5.U5G647   1999
331.7′02—dc21   99–28721
                                                                        CIP

Published by VGM Career Horizons
A division of NTC/Contemporary Publishing Group, Inc.
4255 West Touhy Avenue, Lincolnwood (Chicago), Illinois 60712-1975 U.S.A.
Copyright © 2000 by NTC/Contemporary Publishing Group, Inc.
All rights reserved. No part of this book may be reproduced, stored in a retrieval
system, or transmitted in any form or by any means, electronic, mechanical,
photocopying, recording, or otherwise, without the prior written permission of
NTC/Contemporary Publishing Group, Inc.
Printed in the United States of America
International Standard Book Number: 0-8442-2959-8 (cloth)
                                                          0-8442-2960-1 (paper)
00   01   02   03   04   05   LB   18   17   16   15   14   13   12   11   10   9   8   7   6   5   4   3   2   1

Contents

This book is dedicated to the
memory of my beloved parents,
Sam and Sylvia Lefkovitz,
and the memory of a dear uncle,
Bernard Lefko.

Acknowledgments

The author gratefully acknowledges:

- The numerous professionals who graciously agreed to be profiled in this book

- My dear husband, Larry, for his inspiration and vision

- My children, Sherri, Deborah, Bruce, for their encouragement and love

- Family and close friends—Adrienne, Marty, Mindi, Cary, Michele, Paul, Michele, Alison, Steve, Marci, Steve, Brian, Steven, Jesse, Bertha, and Aunt Helen—for their faith and support

- Diana Catlin, for her insights and input

- Betsy Lancefield, editor at VGM, for making all projects rewarding and enjoyable

CHAPTER ONE

Is the Patriotic Path Right for You?

"Ask not what your country can do for you; ask what you can do for your country." JOHN F. KENNEDY

Does the John F. Kennedy quote above call out to you? For many, the feelings expressed above strike a chord. To these individuals, the patriotic spirit is very strong. Many feel that the best way to carry out this sentiment is through career choice. And that's where this book comes in. It describes a wide range of occupations that will allow you to express the patriotic spirit in your heart.

Is the patriotic path proper for you? Take the following self-test and you'll find out!

The Patriotic Quiz

1. Do you have an especially strong feeling about allegiance to your country?

2. Would you be willing to relocate to another part of the country or even the world?

3. Could you adjust to unconventional work schedules?

4. Are you self-confident about your abilities?

5. Do you have a willingness to serve others and your country?

1

6. Do you enjoy meeting and dealing with many kinds of people?

7. Are you flexible about living conditions—possibly difficult ones?

8. Are you comfortable with an element of danger in your work?

9. Are you willing to make great sacrifices for your country and your fellow men and women?

10. Are you willing to risk your own well-being for the well-being of others?

A Tradition of Patriotism

In a large number of cases, patriotism seems to run in families. Did you know about these presidents' children who also served in the government?

- John Quincy Adams—son of John Adams
  Minister to the Netherlands from 1794 to 1796
  Minister to Germany from 1796 to 1801
  Senator of Massachusetts from 1803 to 1808
  Minister to St. Petersburg from 1809 to 1811
  Negotiator of Treaty of Ghent in 1814
  Minister to Great Britain from 1815 to 1817
  Secretary of State from 1817 to 1825
  President from 1825 to 1829
  Representative from Massachusetts from 1831 to 1848

- Charles Francis Adams—son of John Quincy Adams
  Representative from Massachusetts from 1859 to 1861
  Minister to Great Britain from 1861 to 1868

- John Scott Harrison—son of William Henry Harrison
  Representative from Virginia from 1893 to 1897

- Robert Todd Lincoln—son of Abraham Lincoln
  Secretary of War from 1881 to 1885
  Minister to Great Britain from 1889 to 1893

- James Rudolph Garfield—son of James Garfield
  Secretary of the Interior from 1907 to 1909

- Theodore Roosevelt Jr.—son of Theodore Roosevelt
  Assistant Secretary of the Navy from 1921 to 1924
  Governor of Puerto Rico from 1929 to 1932
  Governor General of the Philippines from 1932 to 1933

- Robert Alphonso Taft—son of William Howard Taft
  Senator from Ohio from 1939 to 1953

- Charles Phelps Taft—son of William Howard Taft
  Mayor of Cincinnati from 1955 to 1957

- Herbert Hoover Jr.—son of Herbert Hoover
  Undersecretary of State for Middle Eastern Affairs from
  1954 to 1957

- Franklin Delano Roosevelt Jr.—son of F.D.R.
  Congressman from New York from 1949 through 1955
  Undersecretary of Commerce from 1963 to 1965
  Chairman of the Equal Employment Opportunity
  Commission from 1965 to 1966

- James Roosevelt—son of F.D.R.
  Representative from California from 1955 to 1965

- Elliott Roosevelt—son of F.D.R.
  Mayor of Miami Beach from 1965 to 1967

- George W. Bush—son of George Bush
  Governor of Texas in 1995 to serve until 2003

- John Ellis (Jeb) Bush—son of George Bush
  Governor of Florida in 1999 to serve until 2003

Fathers and Daughters

Several women followed their fathers in serving the nation as senators and representatives.

- Ruth Hanna McCormick—daughter of Senator Mark Hanna
  Representative from Illinois from 1929 to 1931

- Ruth Bryan Owen—daughter of William Jennings Bryan
  Representative from Florida from 1929 to 1933

- Clare Boothe Luce—stepdaughter of Representative Albert E. Austin
  Representative from Connecticut from 1943 to 1947

- Louise Goff Reece—daughter of Senator Guy Despard Goff
  Representative from Tennessee from 1961 to 1963

- Lucille Roybal-Allard—daughter of Representative Edward Roybal
  Representative from California who began serving in 1993

- Susan Molinari—daughter of Representative Guy Molinari
  Representative from New York from 1990 to 1997

Perhaps you will be the one in your family to initiate this patriotic trend. Or you may follow in the footsteps of other members of your family who have already entered one of the patriotic fields—law enforcement, firefighting, the Peace Corps, the military, careers on foreign soil, politics, or government. All of these areas are open to patriotic souls.

The Patriotic Essence

The essence of patriotism was clearly expressed by President Dwight D. Eisenhower, in words attributed as his last: "I've always loved my wife. I've always loved my children. I've always loved my grandchildren. And I have always loved my country."

CHAPTER TWO

Careers in Law Enforcement

"The execution of the laws is more important than the making of them." THOMAS JEFFERSON

I n recent years, American voters have made it clear that they want government to place greater emphasis on reducing serious crime through law enforcement. In response to this, law enforcement officers are becoming more visible and involved in communities, particularly high-crime, urban neighborhoods. This serves to increase public confidence in the police and mobilizes the public to help police fight crime.

Law Enforcers

Through the use of government, volunteer, and commercial resources, those who enforce the law are encouraging people in the community to help them identify and solve ongoing problems. One focus is to make the police officer a permanent, highly visible figure in the neighborhood rather than merely an officer called in to respond to a crime.

Police Officers

Police officers working in smaller communities and rural areas are usually given varied responsibilities for handling general law enforcement duties. In the course of a day's work, they may investigate a burglary, direct traffic at the scene of a fire, or give first aid to an accident victim. In larger police departments and federal agencies, officers and special agents usually are assigned to a specific detail for a fixed length of time. Some may become experts in chemical and microscopic analysis or handwriting and fingerprint identification. They may also serve as members of the mounted or motorcycle patrol, harbor patrol, canine corps, special weapons and tactics groups, or task forces created to combat specific types of crime.

Most new police recruits begin their careers in an urban setting where they are often initiated by serving on patrol duty, riding in a police vehicle. In smaller agencies, they may work alone; in larger agencies, they ride with experienced officers. Patrols generally cover a specific area, perhaps an old and congested business district or outlying residential neighborhood. Officers strive to become very familiar with conditions throughout their patrol areas and, while on patrol, remain alert for anything unusual. They note suspicious circumstances, such as open windows or lights in vacant buildings, as well as hazards to public safety. Officers on patrol enforce traffic regulations while keeping an eye out for stolen vehicles or wanted individuals. On a preestablished regular basis, officers report to police headquarters by radio or telephone (police can also use a "secure" channel on their radios for confidential information).

Meet Michael Untirdt, Patrol Officer

Thirty-six-year-old Patrolman Michael Untirdt is a member of a village police department located near a large metropolitan city. He has served as a police officer for the past twelve years.

"I became interested in this career at the college level when I began taking courses at Western Illinois University," says Untirdt. "I especially found classes about law interesting, so I made that my major and graduated with a bachelor's degree in law enforcement. Another thing that drew me to this type of work was that I would be out in the streets among the people rather than sitting behind a desk all day. That was very appealing to me.

"During my last semester of college when I was required to complete an internship, I chose to do mine with a police department. I felt this was very valuable because it really gave me a more realistic view of what the job entails. I was exposed to all the shifts, record keeping, radio operation, everything related to being a police officer.

"What's it like to be a police officer? Actually, to some, the daily schedule may seem somewhat boring," says Untirdt. "Ninety percent of the routine involves driving around patrolling—being on the alert for individuals who are breaking the law or who look suspicious and as if they have something to hide. The rest of our time is spent responding to calls from the public and filling out reports.

"Though we are getting busier every year, right now we handle only a few rapes, homicides, and domestic violence calls. So, we must always be ready to proceed in such situations in the event that any come in. If one does, and especially if it is an in-progress call, your adrenaline starts pumping and you begin to think ahead to what your course of action will be when you get close.

"Candidates for this career must meet the requirements set by each agency, which may vary from one to another. Usually, this means a high school degree (although college experience is becoming more and more desirable) and an age requirement (often eighteen or twenty-one). Individuals who successfully pass all tests are sent to police academies. Police academies are fairly standardized, at least within the state of Illinois. Whether you live in downstate Illinois and go to the Police Training Institute in Champaign, the Chicago Police Academy, the State Police Academy, or the Cook County Sheriffs' Academy, you get essentially the same training based on the same curriculum. Chosen candidates attend for ten or twelve weeks, although some recruits may stay a little longer to receive additional instruction that is specific to procedures in their particular police agency.

"Besides formal training at the academy, I believe police officers need to have common sense and the ability to relate well to all kinds of people. This requires them to show compassion, understanding, and a healthy respect for the plight of others. I always treat everyone the way I would like to be treated," stresses Untirdt.

"One way to explore an interest in this career is to look into the ride-along program that most towns offer. Try to take advantage of this opportunity by going along, particularly on differing shifts. Try to put yourself in this police officer's shoes. Ask some questions as you ride along. Imagine yourself doing this kind of work for the next twenty or twenty-five years. Though it may be hard to project yourself so far into the future, this is a good opportunity to find out if police work is truly your calling."

Meet Aric Steven Frazier, Chairperson and Professor of Law Enforcement

Aric Steven Frazier earned an associate's degree in law enforcement at Vincennes University and bachelor's and master's degrees in science (with a major in criminal justice) at the University of Evansville. He also holds several certifications in firearms as a master instructor through the Indiana Law Enforcement Training Board. He has served as a police officer and training officer/director at Indiana State Academy and presently is professor of law enforcement and chairperson of the law enforcement department at Vincennes University.

"First and foremost, I was drawn to this career because I enjoyed working with people," Frazier says. "I have always had an ability to keep people motivated and interested, so I feel that I am effective working in the relationship of trainer/teacher to police officer. I feel that since I enjoy this line of work so much, then others will, too.

"I always wanted to be a police officer," he says. "I know I have a facility to solve problems, and police officers need to do this on a day-to-day basis. And they will continue in this capacity because many people don't seem able to solve their problems on their own, so situations tend to recur.

"I've never felt that police work was dangerous as long as police officers use their heads and their training/education," he continues. "And I feel that it is my responsibility to make others the best police they can be. I enjoy the challenge of taking charge and working together with others as a team.

"I know that injurious things can and do happen but not if we are prepared. I am able to do my job in an effective manner because I am not afraid of anyone. I am not over confident, but fear really doesn't enter my mind.

"I so enjoy my career that I can't wait to get to class to present the material for that day. Sometimes I get physically tired but once I get involved in a lecture, this quickly dissipates. Between consulting, teaching, and also serving as a college/high school basketball official (approximately sixty games a year), my schedule is very busy. And that really makes the days go quickly. Before I know it, another one is over. I need some time off, of course, and enjoy being with my wife and kids during those periods.

"My day starts at 5 A.M. with a good workout. I lift weights and run. From there, I lecture at least four to five hours a day, and, during office hours, I look over traffic cases sent to me by attorneys or insurance companies. If I don't have to go to the scene of an incident, I'll work it up at home instead. If going to the scene is needed, I'll go and get back home ASAP, usually about 9 P.M. to 10 P.M. (and that is true for basketball games too).

"I feel each individual should choose a career that is pleasurable because life is too short not to. I dislike having to have contact with individuals who do not know how to work or to learn. But I very much enjoy working with people who are not necessarily knowledgeable but willing to learn. Those who think they know everything are usually the ones who know little.

"My advice to others would be to work hard and have fun doing it. Be sure to build a foundation by getting an education and *learn* as much as you can. Avoid easy classes and instructors. Seek out the ones that you will learn from. Be sure that this is the career for you—if not, choose another that will make you happy. We all make mistakes in life that we are sorry about. Learn from this mistake and *never* do it again. To err is human; to err twice is stupid. Understand that things don't always go the way you want them to. Work harder and they will. Be confident in yourself and your abilities. No one is like you, so don't try to be someone else. No matter what career you choose, you'll really like yourself more if you stay true to yourself. Have goals and work for them and take care of yourself because no one else will."

Meet Michael A. Beltranena Jr., Director of Police

Michael A. Beltranena Jr. earned his A.A. in police administration from Rider University in Trenton, New Jersey, in 1975. This was followed by a B.S. in police science from Rutgers University in New Brunswick, New Jersey, in 1981 and an M.A. in criminal justice from John Jay College in New York City in 1986.

Also to his credit are the following: New Jersey State Police Basic Municipal Police Academy, Sea Girt, New Jersey, 1972; Nevada Highway Patrol Academy, Stead, Nevada, 1980; F.B.I. National Academy, Quantico, Virginia, 1989; United State Secret Service Dignitary Protection Seminar, Washington, D.C., 1987; Law Enforcement Executive Development Seminar, Quantico, Virginia, 1995. Beltranena now serves as director of police of the New Brunswick Police Department in New Jersey.

"I was attracted to the law enforcement field as a child in Brooklyn, New York, when I would visit the local police station on my way home from school," says Beltranena. "I enjoyed the opportunity to work with people, the excitement, and, of course, helping people whenever I could.

"The most significant experience that had a bearing on my career path was working for a former police director who mentored me and encouraged me to set goals and work towards them. He always told me that I could make a difference and that I should concentrate on learning from others by observing their successes and their mistakes.

"My current job as police director is probably the most fulfilling job I have ever had," Beltranena says. "It is fun, challenging, stressful, but most important, I feel that I am able to lead a police department to provide the best possible service to the community. I work approximately sixty hours per week and enjoy every moment. Even when the stress level is high, I am still having fun and look forward to going to work.

"The most enjoyable part of my work is training younger officers to perform their duties ethically and professionally. I feel that I can make a difference by developing people to take over after I am gone. The downside is when I have to deal with those who have let the agency down by not performing ethically. Another downside is having one of my officers injured. Since they are out there doing the job that I have sent them out to do, I feel responsible when they do not come back the same as when they left the station.

"My advice to anyone who strives to be a police administrator is to be prepared. Continue your career, read as much as you can, adopt a mentor, and, most important, do what you know is the right thing to do."

Meet Richard P. Saunders, Lieutenant/Patrol Commander

Lieutenant/Patrol Commander Richard P. Saunders is a member of the Tohono O'odham Nation of southern Arizona. He is responsible for supervising the operations of the 172-member Tohono O'odham Nation Police Department (TOPD) in Sells, Arizona, which serves 23,000 tribe members.

The TOPD is responsible for the investigation of all offenses occurring on the Tohono O'odham Nation reservation with the exception of criminal homicides involving Native Americans, which is handled by the Federal Bureau of Investigation. Traffic and criminal violations involving Native Americans are contested in tribal court. Felony violations involving Native Americans are contested in federal court. All violations committed by non-Native Americans, where Native American people or properties are involved, are contested in state courts.

Saunders earned an Arizona Law Enforcement Officers Advisory Council Peace Officer Certification in 1987. His background also includes one thousand hours of law-related course work and training leading to certification (criminal, traffic, tribal, state, and federal laws); Bureau of Indian Affairs Supervisory Certification, Artesia, New Mexico, 1994; and certification as a Gang Resistance Education and Training Instructor, GREAT, 1994, General Instructor Certified with an emphasis on physical fitness.

"I was recruited by a fellow tribe member working as a police officer for the Tohono O'odham Nation," Saunders says. "He told me of a very challenging and responsible career in the law enforcement profession. I saw this as an opportunity to serve my own people and work within the boundaries of my reservation while enforcing laws and protecting lives. My ability to speak the Tohono O'odham language proved to be invaluable in my daily contacts with people.

"I started in 1996 as a first-line supervisor. Later that year, I was promoted to patrol lieutenant in charge of the patrol division, recruiting and implementing community-oriented policing concepts. I served seven years as a patrol officer responding to calls for service within the Tohono O'odham Nation.

"Today, as a member of upper management, I assist with key decision making in the patrol operations of our department and am responsible for the recruitment and hiring of police officers. My job requires me to be on call twenty-four hours a day. I normally spend anywhere from ten to twelve hours a day on the job.

"The Tohono O'odham Nation is comprised of 2.8 million acres, the same size as the state of Connecticut. We are located sixty miles west of the city of Tucson. Currently, we have eighty certified police officers that patrol eleven districts of our nation, two of which are separate from the main reservation and are located near a metropolitan area. In addition, we have approximately sixty-three miles of the international boundary separating our nation, the country of Mexico, and the United States. As a result of this boundary, we have an influx of illegal contraband and aliens from Mexico. A typical load of illegal drugs is worth anywhere from $1,000 to hundreds of thousands of dollars.

"My daily duties include meeting with tribal elected leaders in the legislative branch to appraise them of our operations and to submit budget requests for funding, meeting with personnel in the judicial branch in order to coordinate cases and resolve detention issues, and meeting with elected leaders from the eleven political districts that comprise the Tohono O'odham Nation. In the case of those districts located off the main reservation, we must assist them with police protection by negotiating memorandums of understanding with neighboring non-Indian police departments such as the Pima and Maricopa County Sheriff's Offices. I meet with tribal governmental departments such as Health and Human Services, attorney general, prosecutors, and so forth, and with nontribal governmental agencies such as the U.S. Border Patrol and U.S. Customs Service to discuss ongoing issues relative to the international boundary. I receive citizens' complaints and work with our staff to resolve these matters in order to promote positive public relations with the community we serve. Due to an increase in juvenile crimes, we promote youth prevention activities and awareness to parents and school staff and administration.

"My position includes many other regularly scheduled meetings. Twice a month, I meet with our supervisors to communicate departmental policies, procedures, and directives. This allows for the sharing of information. Twice a week I meet with the chief of police in our regular upper management meetings. We discuss departmental goals and objectives in order to improve professional services to the community. Once a month I am required to attend a weekend community meeting in one of the eleven districts. These meetings also take place during regular and after-work hours. As in a town hall forum, I listen to public concerns and obtain community input while sharing the direction of the department. This is where my ability to speak the Tohono O'od-ham language is most beneficial.

"Another part of my responsibility is to process payroll and authorize overtime for the entire department. This is a very tedious and time-consuming task.

"The work atmosphere is stressful and intense due to the critical nature of law enforcement. What I like the most about my work is the opportunity to meet people and to learn from top administrators who have had extensive experience in this profession. This allows me to grow and develop my skills as I advance the career ladder.

"The advice I would give to someone wanting to follow in my footsteps would be to identify a mentor with strong leadership experience. Have a dream and set both short- and long-term goals. Believe in yourself and strive toward achieving those goals. With hard work, dedication, and commitment, the goals you set for yourself shall be fulfilled."

Sheriffs and Deputy Sheriffs

In rural areas or wherever there is no local police department, sheriffs and deputy sheriffs are the ones who enforce the law and serve the legal processes of courts. Sheriffs' duties resemble those of local or county police departments but generally on a smaller scale. In most cases, fewer than twenty-five deputies are on staff; in some cases the number is perhaps ten or fewer.

Detectives and Special Agents

Detectives and special agents work as plainclothes investigators, gathering facts and collecting evidence for criminal cases. They conduct interviews, examine records, observe the activities of suspects, and participate in raids or arrests.

Special agents employed by the United States Department of Justice may work for the Drug Enforcement Administration, the Federal Bureau of Investigation, the United States Border Patrol, or the United States Marshals Service. Drug Enforcement Administration (DEA) special agents specialize in enforcement of drug laws and regulations. Agents may conduct complex criminal investigations, carry out surveillance of criminals, and infiltrate illicit drug organizations using undercover techniques. They may work closely with confidential sources of information to collect evidence leading to the seizure of assets gained from the sale of illegal drugs.

Regardless of where they work, police, detectives, and special agents spend considerable time writing reports and maintaining records. When their arrests result in legal action, they are usually called in to testify in court. Some senior officers, such as chief inspectors, commanders, division and bureau chiefs, and agents in charge, have administrative and supervisory duties and are responsible for the operation of geographic divisions of an agency, certain kinds of criminal investigations, and various agency functions.

Police, detectives, and special agents usually work a forty-hour week, but paid overtime work is common. Since police protection must be provided around the clock, several work shifts are necessary. Law enforcers with less seniority are most likely to work weekends, holidays, and nights. Police officers, detectives, and special agents are subject to call at any time their services are needed and may work long hours during criminal investigations.

The jobs of some special agents, such as United States Secret Service and DEA special agents, require extensive travel, often on very short notice.

Some police, detectives, and special agents with agencies such as the United States Border Patrol have to work outdoors for long periods in all kinds of weather.

While police work is inherently dangerous, good training, teamwork, and equipment such as bullet-resistant vests minimize the number of injuries and fatalities. The risks associated with pursuing speeding motorists, apprehending criminals, and dealing with public disorders can be very stressful for the officer as well as for his or her family.

Meet Kevin Illia, FBI Special Agent

Kevin Illia is a special agent with the FBI who serves as a recruiter in the FBI's Chicago office. Born and raised in San Francisco, he spent four years in the United States Air Force. Two of those were spent in Southeast Asia during the Vietnam War. Subsequent to this, he went back to school, earned his bachelor's degree from Sonoma State College in California and his master's degree in public affairs from Washington University in St. Louis.

"In the twenty-four years I've been with the FBI, I've served in all parts of the country," Illia says. "For two and one-half of those years, I was in charge of an antiterrorist team in San Juan, Puerto Rico, and, for the past fifteen, I've been assigned to the Chicago office.

"Always interested in police and fire fighting, it was natural that I take up this career. When I was in the air force serving in a military police unit, we had a warehouse robbery involving about a half a million dollars worth of stolen equipment. An FBI agent assigned to the case solved it in about two hours, and I was so impressed that I decided this was the career for me. The follow-up to the story is that the agent surmised the robbery was undoubtedly an 'inside job' because the warehouse was isolated on the base. He instructed us to gather together all the personnel who worked in that warehouse (a total of ten to fifteen people) and interviewed them until he was able to elicit a confession from two or three of them. We located the stolen property the same night. Case closed.

"As the largest federal investigative agency in the government (more than 10,800 special agents—both male and female) we investigate more than 280 violations in federal laws. These span everything from the more well-known violations such as bank robbery (of which we've had a record twenty-two in the past week here), to kidnappings, civil rights violations, environmental crimes, fair housing infractions, and even violations of the migratory bird act. Anything involving interstate commerce is also in our jurisdiction. In addition, we also cover foreign counterintelligence work and any type of domestic terrorism, such as the Twin Towers bombing in New York City a few years ago at the World Trade Center. We also handle crime on the high seas. (We've had cases where people have been murdered on cruise ships, and, if they're outside the territorial waters of the United States but it's an American carrier, that's still our jurisdiction.) For me and many others, a great part of the appeal of the job is the variety of violations we deal with. If you get tired of dealing with one thing, you can move to another squad that is handling an entirely different type of violation.

"We train all of our agents to be investigators. That is their primary responsibility regardless of what their academic backgrounds are. A new agent who comes in as a lawyer or an accountant will go through the same sixteen-week training at the FBI Academy at Quantico, Virginia, as a military officer or school teacher does. This fact gives continuity to our organization—a common bond of training.

"Once someone applies, he or she will go through our screening procedure. Phase one is the written examination, which includes math and English, situational judgment, and cognitive questions. We need to ascertain if candidates have analytical skills and common sense sufficient to make them capable of making good choices in a variety of situations. If they pass these tests, they'll move to the oral interview, what we call an assessment interview. Individuals appear and answer questions asked by a board of three special agents. If they pass that, we give them drug and polygraph tests. During this, we'll ask them about the veracity of the information they provided us in their applications. We ask questions about drugs and issues of contact with any foreign intelligence services or terrorist organizations, for example. (This is important because the type of information we handle could be of value to other agencies and organizations that do not have the welfare and best interests of the United States in mind.) Those who pass that phase move to the background investigation phase. For this, we go back ten years based on the information they provide us. Once they work through the system and successfully complete the process, we'll offer them an appointment at the FBI Academy as a special agent candidate.

"I'd like to describe what a typical day is like for an FBI agent, but there is no such thing. Most of the time, the plans you make are disrupted by some event that comes up unexpectedly. For instance, last Friday I was prepared to fulfill an obligation to give a presentation to some students. Then a case came up involving a fellow who had killed two individuals. Our fugitive squad was going out and needed some people, so I accompanied them. With search warrant in hand, we scoured his house and found him underneath the bathroom basin. This was a trick in itself because there are a lot of pipes under the basin and the man was six feet tall. He had his feet wrapped around the pipes somehow, as if he was a contortionist. The point is—you never know what your day will bring. Recently, we've had a rash of bank robberies and can be called out any time during the day to interview witnesses (or related individuals) or to appear in court to testify or appear before a grand jury.

"Another aspect of this career is that you never know where you may be called upon to travel to. A few years ago, I was working on an investigation of public corruption in Chicago and had mentioned that I'd worked in Puerto Rico. Subsequently, I got a call that they needed some people who knew the island. I was asked to leave the very next day. I thought it would be only a week, so I agreed to leave my division here in Chicago to help out down there. The week turned into two months.

"This brings me to mentioning what qualities I think are important for FBI agents. As I just pointed out in the Puerto Rico story, you really have to be flexible and have a desire for adventure. It's also important to maintain a sense of humor, have integrity, and be a self-starter. Perseverance and tenacity are also desirable. We seek individuals who are interested in making a contribution to their communities, their nation, their society. We want people who are loyal, patriotic, and who are willing to make sacrifices. It's likely that you'll be relocated to another part of the country and may have to work weekends and even holidays sometimes. I've missed at least three Christmases and four Thanksgivings in my twenty-four year career. That can be difficult on any individual.

"I think the more skills you bring to the FBI, the greater the opportunities for your employment. For instance, we give preference to attorneys, accountants, linguists (individuals fluent in Mandarin Chinese or Spanish, for example), individuals with scuba certification, those with private pilot licenses, paramedic certification, and/or advanced degrees. The more skills you have, the more valuable you are and the more competitive a candidate you will be. But you must have patience—a good deal of patience, perhaps. The process is sometimes slow and quite lengthy. Despite this, we still see continuing eagerness by large numbers of people who send us applications. In fact, this year we were asked to hire 640 special agents nationwide. As of last week, applications submitted to fifty-six field offices throughout the United States totaled thirty-five thousand. Though the numbers are formidable, I encourage you to contact one of the FBI offices in your area for more information. We have applicant units in fifty-six field offices along with smaller satellites called resident offices. Any agency can refer you to our main divisional applicant units. We are always happy to help prospective candidates. I invite all of you to join us!"

Meet Kenneth Rewers, Explosives Technician

Detective Kenneth Rewers is an explosives technician and director of the bomb squad for the Cook County Sheriff's Police Department in Illinois.

"My career began twenty-five years ago as a patrol officer," says Rewers. "The first two years were spent on patrol before I went into a task force assignment (a squad that was put together for problem areas), then to the detective section (crimes against property), then to homicide robbery for about five or six years, then to security detail for the state's attorney for six and one-half years, and then with the sheriff assigned to a security detail and running the bomb squad, where I am now.

"Much of why I'm here today is a result of something that happened one Saturday afternoon when I was working in the detective section out of our Homewood facility. Someone walked in with a pipe bomb. The desk officer told him that the detectives handle all that, so the man with the bomb walked in and laid it on my desk. I had absolutely no idea what to do, but fortunately there was one police officer on duty who had a military background and some expertise with bombs. We got him in to handle it, and that took care of that.

"Predicated on that incident and a number of others that were similar, we decided that it would be wise to set up a separate bomb unit. So, I was one of the first to attend the FBI training center in Huntsville, Alabama, where all the bomb technicians in the United States and some foreign facilities are now trained. After completing a three-and-a-half-week initial training, you become certified as an explosives technician. Every fifteen to eighteen months following that, you are required to attend a one-week refresher course. In addition, our squad members train together once a week in order to share our experiences and stay on top of the most recent developments in this field.

"All of our people work full-time now because of the number of calls for service—in excess of three hundred last year. Illinois ranks second behind California in the number of bomb incidents that occur. Fortunately, the administration supports us with the equipment we need, which is, indeed, very expensive.

"Our basic requirement is that you serve five years with the police department first, and then you may apply for an explosives position. Individuals must realize that it is expensive for the federal government to train individuals for this kind of work, and, as a result, you must make a five-year commitment to be a part of one of these units.

"When we are interested in adding personnel to our explosives division, I place a notice so that those who are interested in pursuing this will get in touch with me. It is well known that our screening procedure is quite intensive and extensive. There are a number of phases in this process that candidates will need to pass successfully, but the one that is foremost is the interview. Because the element of trust is so vital, all members of the squad attend to share in the decision of whether or not a candidate should be accepted.

"Once candidates are accepted, they will probably wait approximately a year and a half before having the opportunity to attend school because only twenty can attend at one time. However, the program is repeated about five or six times a year. Even friendly foreign governments send some of their people over here to attend school because it's about the only type that I know of in the nation, in fact in the world.

"You'd be surprised at the situations we are called in to handle. We get a lot of pipe bomb cases, particularly associated with kids who are experimenting with various types of explosives. Just recently I was involved with one high school that performed a routine check of students' lockers and found an individual who had numerous books on how to build explosive devices. The local police called us. We went out there and spoke with the youth and then to his parents. The upshot of the story is that three devices were in the house already, and the parents had no idea that any of this was going on. If any of the devices had exploded, the power would have been sufficient to take the young boy's hand off.

"One important decision we must always make is whether or not to neutralize the devices right on the spot or move them somewhere else. You have to evaluate the potential risks involved either or both ways. We do have transporters that help us to move devices; still, you're taking the chance of shaking or disturbing them in trying to move them to a safer place.

"They say dogs are a man's best friend, and that's true for explosives handlers for sure, especially the explosives dogs that are trained to pick up on the scent of even the smallest bit of nitrates. From there, a technician will take over. Similar to canines who are able to sniff out drugs, these animals do a wonderful job of detecting the explosives without even disturbing the package. They are truly amazing and we very much appreciate their help," stresses Rewers.

"We train with other agencies and belong to the Great Lakes Bomb Tech Association, which includes Chicago and all the other major squads in the surrounding area. Every other month, we meet for a training session during which we'll go over problems that have occurred with devices since our last meeting. In so doing, we share information and alert one another to potential problems. We also run sessions for local police departments in order to acquaint them with the proper procedures they should use for dealing with bombs—at least until we can get there and take over. We also work very closely with the Alcohol, Tobacco, and Firearms (ATF) unit, which is the investigative agency that will handle explosives cases.

"Safety is always our main concern," stresses Rewers. "You have to make the right decisions at the outset. This means that you must quickly and carefully assess the situation, confer with your partner, and decide the approach you're going to take. A mistake can bring tragic results. You may not get a second chance. But, even with that said, and knowing the dangers involved, we who have chosen this career find it to be both interesting and challenging."

Meet David Jenkins, SWAT Team Member

David Jenkins, a twenty-year year law enforcement veteran, is a member of the Northern Illinois Police Alarm System (NIPAS), a Special Weapons and Tactics (SWAT) team.

"My father was a marine for twenty-six years, so it was not unusual that I would follow suit," says Jenkins. "I entered the military at nineteen and served three years in the Vietnam War as a Green Beret. As a light heavy-weapons specialist, I served as a teacher. Our unit went in behind enemy lines to train other personnel how to engage in guerrilla-type warfare. Following that, I came to Illinois with my wife, who was expecting our first child. I got a job doing security and juvenile work for School District 214 and stayed on there for three years.

"In 1975, I was hired to work as a tactical officer for the police department, and I served three years in the detective's bureau. Subsequently, I served as a patrol officer. I've been a member of the SWAT team for the past seven years—three as part of the entry team (a team of ten who are trained to go in first), then a member of the marksman (or sniper) team for about a year and a half, and then in tactical intelligence doing background information and training for the fifty-member team.

"When SWAT teams are called in, the situations are all potentially dangerous, otherwise they would have been handled by the local law enforcement community. Our particular SWAT team represents a unique situation in that it is a blending of team members from seventy-five towns. The group is combined in order to have a substantial team that is then at the disposal of any of the seventy-five member towns.

"Anyone interested in SWAT team work must have experience as a police officer first. In our department, you need to have at least five years of experience on the street before you can even consider applying. Individuals who are interested go through a rigorous selection process before the most desirable candidates are chosen and assigned to training. The screenings include a physical agility test and psychological tests. Those who pass that go into a two-week basic training period with the NIPAS team. Training continues in an on-going fashion throughout the year.

"There is no full-time SWAT team, so we are called in when there is a serious situation that other law enforcers are not equipped to handle—for example, natural disasters, drug raids serving high-risk warrants, hostage situations, or riots.

"SWAT team members are on call twenty-four hours a day, seven days a week. Each team member carries a pager, and, if a situation occurs and the team is called out, members are notified by the dispatch center, which puts out a message via our pagers.

"The SWAT service has nothing to do with working our regular shifts as police professionals in our regular assignments. If a situation comes up during a shift, I immediately grab my gear and head to the SWAT destination. If they need to replace me, they will send someone to take my regular assignment. If I am home, I have to have my pager on at all times. If they call me out during the night, I just respond to the incident from my home.

"We've had to contend with individuals brandishing machetes, kids building bombs and threatening to blow themselves up, individuals with rifles who are threatening family members or other people. We've been called to locations where individuals have actually been in the process of shooting people and barricading themselves, sometimes with and sometimes without hostages. We never know what we'll be called up to handle.

"SWAT work is very demanding. You must do a lot of sacrificing. In the seven years I've spent on the team, I trained and handled emergencies on my own time, and it's taxing on the family sometimes. Wives and significant others sometimes have a hard time dealing with the danger, watching their loved ones being called out in the middle of the night, not knowing what's going on until the situation is resolved, one way or the other. You must really have your personal life in order because there's a lot of responsibility to this job.

"When we are able to handle a situation without firing a shot, we consider that a successful resolution. All law enforcers are interested in protecting and serving, and we want everyone to go home safe and sound. If things work out that way, we have truly fulfilled our goal."

United States Marshals

United States marshals and deputy marshals provide security for the federal courts, including judges, witnesses, and prisoners. They apprehend fugitives and operate the Special Operations Group (SOG), a tactical unit that responds to high-threat and emergency situations. Some deputies provide security to the Department of Defense and the United States Air Force during movements of missiles between military facilities.

Border Patrol Officers

United States Border Patrol officers are responsible for protecting more than eight thousand miles of international land and water boundaries. Their primary mission is to detect and prevent the smuggling and unlawful entry of undocumented aliens into the United States and to apprehend those persons found in violation of the immigration laws. The Border Patrol is the primary agency operating along the land borders between the ports of entry for illicit drugs and various contraband. They accomplish their mission through activities such as tracking, traffic checks on roads and highways leading away from the border, and participating in various task force operations with other law enforcement agencies.

Special Agents

Special agents employed by the United States Department of the Treasury work for the Bureau of Alcohol, Tobacco, and Firearms (BATF), the United States Customs Service, Internal Revenue Service, and United States Secret Service. Bureau of Alcohol, Tobacco, and Firearms special agents investigate violations of federal explosives laws, including bombings and arson-for-profit schemes affecting interstate commerce. They may investigate suspected illegal sales, possession, or use of firearms. Other BATF agents investigate violations related to the illegal sale of liquor and interstate smuggling of untaxed cigarettes. These investigations involve surveillance, participation in raids, interviewing suspects, and searching for physical evidence. Customs agents enforce laws to prevent smuggling of goods across United States borders. Internal Revenue Service special agents collect evidence against individuals and companies that are evading the payment of federal taxes.

United States Secret Service special agents are charged with two main missions—protection and investigation. During the course of their careers, they may be assigned to protect the president and vice president and their immediate families, presidential candidates, former presidents, and foreign dignitaries visiting the United States. Secret Service agents also investigate counterfeiting, the forgery of government checks or bonds, and the fraudulent use of credit cards.

Special agents employed by the United States Department of State work for the Diplomatic Security Service. Diplomatic Security Service special agents advise ambassadors on security matters and manage a complex range of security programs overseas. In the United States, they investigate passport and visa fraud, conduct personnel security investigations, issue security clearances, and protect the Secretary of State and certain foreign dignitaries. They train foreign civilian police, who then return to their own countries better able to fight terrorism.

Various other federal agencies employ special agents with sworn police powers and the authority to carry firearms and make arrests. These agencies generally evolved from the need for security for the agency's property and personnel. The largest such agency is the Federal Protective Service, which has personnel nationwide. Other examples include the United States Mint police, the Government Printing Service police, and the Central Intelligence Agency's Special Protective Service.

State Troopers

State police officers (sometimes called state troopers or highway patrol officers) patrol our highways and enforce motor vehicle laws and regulations by issuing traffic citations to motorists who are in violation of the law. Called in to help at the scene of an accident, they may direct traffic, give first aid, and/or call for emergency equipment. They also write reports that may be used to determine the cause of the accident. In addition, state police officers may provide services to motorists on the highways, such as calling for road service for drivers with mechanical trouble.

State police also enforce criminal laws. They are frequently called upon to render assistance to officers of other law enforcement agencies. In rural areas that do not have a police force or a local representative from the sheriff's department, the state police are the primary law enforcement agency, investigating any crimes that occur, such as burglary or assault.

Qualifications and Training Required for Law Enforcers

The appointment of police personnel and detectives is governed by civil service regulations in most states and large cities—and even in some smaller ones. Candidates for these positions must be United States citizens, generally at least twenty years old, and must meet rigorous physical and personal qualifications. Eligibility for appointment generally depends on education, experience, and successful performance on competitive written examinations. In addition, physical examinations often include tests of vision, hearing, strength, and agility.

Because personal characteristics such as honesty, judgment, integrity, and a sense of responsibility are especially important in law enforcement work, candidates are interviewed by senior officers, and their character traits and background are investigated. In some agencies, candidates are interviewed by a psychiatrist or a psychologist or given a personality test. Most applicants are subjected to lie detector examinations and drug testing. (And some agencies subject sworn personnel to random drug testing as a condition of continuing employment.) Although police, detectives, and special agents work independently, they must perform their duties in accordance with the law and departmental rules.

In larger police departments, where the majority of law enforcement jobs are found, applicants usually must have at least a high school education. Increasingly, local, special, and state departments require at least some college training and certainly prefer it. Virtually all federal agencies require a college degree.

Many junior colleges, colleges, and universities offer programs in law enforcement or administration of justice. Other courses helpful in preparing for a career in law enforcement include accounting, finance, electrical engineering or computer science, and foreign languages. Knowledge of a foreign language is an asset in many agencies. Physical education and sports are helpful in developing the competitiveness, stamina, and agility needed for law enforcement work.

Some large cities hire high school graduates who are still in their teens as police cadets or trainees. They do clerical work and attend classes and can be appointed to the regular force at the conclusion of their training, usually in one to two years, upon reaching the minimum age requirement.

The federal agency with the largest number of special agents is the Federal Bureau of Investigation (FBI). To be considered for appointment as an FBI special agent, an applicant either must be a graduate of an accredited law school, a college graduate with a major in accounting, or a college graduate with either fluency in a foreign language or three years of full-time work experience. Applicants must be United States citizens, possess a valid driver's license, be between twenty-three and thirty-seven years of age at the time of appointment, and be willing to accept an assignment anywhere in the United States. They also must be in excellent physical condition with vision at least corrected to 20/40 in one eye and 20/20 in the other eye. All new agents undergo sixteen weeks of training at the FBI academy on the United States Marine Corps base in Quantico, Virginia.

Applicants for special agent jobs with the United States Department of Treasury's Secret Service and BATF must have a bachelor's degree or a minimum of three years' work experience that demonstrates the ability to deal effectively with individuals or groups, collect and assemble pertinent facts, and prepare clear and concise reports. Candidates must be in excellent physical condition and be less than thirty-seven years of age at the time they enter the agency unless they have previous qualifying federal law enforcement experience. Prospective special agents undergo eight weeks of training at the Federal Law Enforcement Training Center in Glynco, Georgia, and another eight to eleven weeks of specialized training with their particular agencies.

Applicants for special agent jobs with the United States Drug Enforcement Administration must be United States citizens, have a college degree in any field, and either one year of experience conducting criminal investigations, one year of graduate school, or have achieved at least a 2.95 grade point average while in college. The minimum age for entry is twenty-one, and the maximum age is thirty-seven, unless the applicant has previous qualifying federal law enforcement experience. DEA special agents undergo fourteen weeks of specialized training at the FBI Academy in Quantico, Virginia.

Before their first assignments, officers usually go through a training period. In small agencies, recruits often get on-the-job training with more experienced officers, rather than formal training. In state and large local departments, they get training at a police academy for twelve to fourteen weeks, as mandated by the state. This training includes classroom instruction in constitutional law and civil rights, state laws and local ordinances, and accident investigation. Recruits also receive training and supervised experience in patrol techniques, traffic control, use of firearms, self-defense, first aid, and handling emergencies.

Police officers usually become eligible for promotion after a probationary period ranging from six months to three years. In a large department, promotion may enable an officer to become a detective or specialize in one type of police work, such as laboratory analysis of evidence, traffic control, communications, or working with juveniles. Promotions to sergeant, lieutenant, and captain are usually very competitive and made according to a candidate's position on a promotion list, as determined by scores on a written examination and on-the-job performance.

Continuing training helps police officers, detectives, and special agents improve their job performance. Through police department academies, regional centers for public safety employees established by the states, and federal agency training centers, instructors provide annual training in defensive tactics, firearms, use-of-force policies, sensitivity and communications skills, crowd-control techniques, legal developments that affect their work, and advances in law enforcement equipment. Many agencies pay all or part of the tuition required for officers to work toward degrees in law enforcement, police science, administration of justice, or public administration and subsequently pay higher salaries to those who earn such a degree.

Job Settings

About 81 percent of the 682,000 individuals employed as police officers, detectives, and special agents work in local governments, primarily in cities with more than 25,000 residents. Some cities have very large police forces, while hundreds of small communities employ fewer than twenty-five officers each. State police agencies employ about 13 percent of all police, detectives, and special agents; various federal agencies employ 6 percent. There are about 17,000 federal, state, special (such as park police, transit police, and county police), and local police agencies in the nation.

Salaries

The median salary of nonsupervisory police officers and detectives is about $34,700 a year. The middle 50 percent earn between $25,700 and $45,300; the lowest 10 percent are paid less than $19,200, while the highest 10 percent earn over

$58,500 a year. Generally, salaries tend to be higher in urban, more affluent jurisdictions, which usually have the best-funded police departments.

In a recent survey, police officers and detectives in supervisory positions reported a median salary of approximately $41,200 a year. The middle 50 percent earned between $29,200 and $33,400 a year; the lowest 10 percent were paid less than $22,500, while the highest 10 percent earned more than $64,500 annually.

Sheriffs and other law enforcement officers had a median annual salary of about $26,700. The middle 50 percent earned between about $20,300 and $37,800; the lowest 10 percent were paid less than $15,900, while the highest 10 percent earned more than $48,400.

Federal law provides special salary rates to federal employees who serve in law enforcement. Additionally, many federal special agents receive administratively uncontrolled overtime (AUO), equal to 25 percent of the agent's grade and step, awarded because of the large amount of overtime that these agents are expected to work. For example, in 1996 FBI agents started at a base salary of $33,800 a year, ultimately earning $42,250 a year with availability pay. Other U.S. Justice and Treasury Department special agents started at about $25,000 or $30,700 a year, therefore earning $31,300 or $38,400 per year, including availability pay, depending on their qualifications. Salaries of federal special agents progressed to $55,600, including availability pay, while supervisory agents started at $66,100, including availability pay. Salaries were slightly higher in selected areas where the prevailing local pay level was higher. Since federal agents may be eligible for a special law enforcement benefits package, applicants should ask their recruiters for more information.

Total earnings for local, state, and special police detectives frequently exceed the stated salary due to payments for overtime, which can be significant. In addition to the common benefits, most police and sheriffs' departments provide officers with special allowances for uniforms and furnish weapons, handcuffs, and other required equipment. In addition, because police officers generally are covered by liberal pension plans, many retire at half-pay after twenty or twenty-five years of service.

For Additional Information

Information about entrance requirements may be obtained from Federal, state, and local law enforcement agencies. Further information about qualifications for employment as an FBI Special Agent is available from the nearest state FBI office. Address and phone number are listed in the local telephone directory.

Information about career opportunities, qualifications, and training to become a deputy marshal is available from:

United States Marshals Service
Employment and Compensation Division
Field Staffing Branch
600 Army Navy Drive
Arlington, VA 22202

Information on careers as a Drug Enforcement Administration special agents may be obtained from:

Drug Enforcement Administration
Special Agent Staffing Unit
Washington, DC 20537

An overview of career opportunities, qualifications, and training for United States Secret Service Special Agents is available from:

Secret Service, Personnel
1800 G Street NW
Washington, DC 20223

Correctional Officers

Correctional officers are charged with overseeing individuals who have been arrested, are awaiting trial or other hearing, or who have been convicted of a crime and sentenced to serve time in a jail, reformatory, or penitentiary. They maintain security and observe inmate conduct and behavior to prevent disturbances and escapes.

Many correctional officers work in small county and municipal jails or precinct station houses as deputy sheriffs or police officers with wide-ranging responsibilities. Others are assigned to large state and federal prisons where job duties are more specialized. A relatively small number supervise aliens being held by the Immigration and Naturalization Service before being released or deported. Regardless of the setting, correctional officers maintain order within the institution and enforce rules and regulations.

To make sure inmates are orderly and obey rules, correctional officers monitor inmates' activities, including working, exercising, eating, and bathing. They assign and supervise inmates' work assignments. Sometimes it is necessary to search inmates and their living quarters for weapons or drugs, to settle disputes between inmates, and to enforce discipline. Correctional officers cannot show favoritism and must report any inmate who violates the rules. A few officers hold staff security positions in towers, where they are equipped with high-powered rifles. Other, unarmed officers are responsible for direct supervision of inmates. They are locked in a cell block alone or with another officer among the fifty to one hundred inmates who reside there. The officers enforce regulations primarily through their communications skills and moral authority.

Other correctional officers periodically inspect the facilities. They may, for example, check cells and other areas of the institution for unsanitary conditions, weapons, drugs, fire hazards, and any evidence of infractions of rules. In addition, they routinely inspect locks, window bars, grille doors, and gates for signs of tampering.

Correctional officers report orally and in writing on inmate conduct and quality and quantity of work done by inmates. Officers also report disturbances, violations of rules, and any unusual occurrences. They usually keep a daily record of their activities. In the most modern facilities, correctional officers can monitor the activities of prisoners from a centralized control center with the aid of closed-circuit television cameras and a computer tracking system. In such an environment, the inmates may not see anyone but officers for days or weeks at a time.

Depending on the offender's classification within the institution, correctional officers may escort inmates to and from cells and other areas and admit and accompany authorized visitors to see inmates. Officers may also escort prisoners between the institution and courtrooms, medical facilities, and other destinations. They inspect mail and visitors for contraband (prohibited items). Should the situation arise, they assist law enforcement authorities by investigating crimes committed within their institution and by helping search for escaped inmates.

Correctional officers may arrange a change in a daily schedule so that an inmate can visit the library, help inmates get news of their families, or help inmates in other ways. In a few institutions, officers receive specialized training, have a more formal counseling role, and may lead or participate in group counseling sessions.

Correctional sergeants directly supervise correctional officers and are responsible for the safety and well-being of the individuals in their keeping. They usually are responsible for maintaining security and directing the activities of a group of inmates during an assigned watch or in an assigned area.

Correctional officers may work indoors or outdoors, depending on their specific duties. Some indoor areas of correctional institutions are well lighted, heated, and ventilated, but others are overcrowded, hot, and noisy. Outdoors, weather conditions may be disagreeable, for example when standing watch on a guard tower in cold weather. Working in a correctional institution can be stressful and hazardous; correctional officers occasionally have been injured or killed by inmates.

Correctional officers usually work an eight-hour day, five-day week, on rotating shifts. Prison security must be provided around the clock, which often means that junior officers work weekends, holidays, and nights. In addition, officers may be required to work overtime.

Qualifications and Training for Correctional Officers

Most institutions require that correctional officers be at least eighteen or twenty-one years of age, have a high school education or its equivalent, have no felony convictions, and be a United States citizen. In addition, correctional institutions increasingly seek correctional officers with postsecondary education, particularly in psychology, criminal justice, police science, criminology, and related fields.

Correctional officers must be in good health. The federal system and many states require candidates to meet formal standards of physical fitness, eyesight, and hearing. Strength, good judgment, and the ability to think and act quickly are indispensable. Other common requirements include a driver's license and work experience that demonstrates reliability. The federal system and some states screen applicants for drug abuse and require candidates to pass a written or oral examination, along with a background check.

Federal, state, and local departments of corrections provide training for correctional officers based on guidelines established by the American Correctional Association, the American Jail Association, and other professional organizations. Some states have special training academies. All states and local departments of correction provide informal on-the-job training at the conclusion of formal instruction. On-the-job trainees receive several weeks or months of training in an actual job setting under an experienced officer.

Academy trainees generally receive instruction on institutional policies, regulations, and operations; constitutional law and cultural awareness; crisis intervention, inmate behavior, and contraband control; custody and security procedures; fire and safety; inmate rules and legal rights; administrative responsibilities; written and oral communication, including preparation of reports; self-defense, including the use of firearms and physical force; first aid, including cardiopulmonary resuscitation (CPR); and physical fitness training. New federal correctional officers must undergo 200 hours of formal training within the first year of employment. They must complete 120 hours of specialized correctional instruction at the Federal Bureau of Prisons residential training center at Glynco, Georgia, within the first sixty days after appointment. Experienced officers receive in-service training to keep abreast of new ideas and procedures.

Entry requirements and on-the-job training vary widely from agency to agency. For instance, correctional officers in North Dakota need two years of college with emphasis on criminal justice or behavioral science or three years as a correctional, military police, or licensed peace officer. The department then provides eighty hours of training at the start and follows up with forty hours of training annually. On the other hand, Connecticut requires only that candidates be eighteen years of age, have a high school diploma or GED certificate, and pass medical and physical examinations, including drug screening. It then provides 520 hours of initial training and follows up with forty hours annually.

Correctional officers have the opportunity to join prison tactical response teams, which are trained to respond to riots, hostage situations, forced cell moves, and other potentially dangerous confrontations. Team members often receive monthly training and practice with weapons, chemical agents, forced entry methods, and other tactics.

With education, experience, and training, qualified officers may advance to correctional sergeant or other supervisory or administrative positions. Many correctional institutions require experience as a correctional officer for other corrections positions. Ambitious correctional officers can be promoted up to assistant warden. Officers sometimes transfer to related areas, such as probation and parole officer.

Job Settings

Correctional officers hold about 310,000 jobs. Six of every ten work at state correctional institutions such as prisons, prison camps, and reformatories. Most of the remainder work at city and county jails or other institutions run by local governments. About nine thousand correctional officers work at federal correctional institutions, and about four thousand work in privately owned and managed prisons.

Most correctional officers work in relatively large institutions located in rural areas, although a significant number work in jails and other smaller facilities located in law enforcement agencies throughout the country.

Salaries

According to a recent survey in *Corrections Compendium*, a national journal for corrections professionals, starting salaries of state correctional officers averaged about $19,100 a year, ranging from $13,700 in Kentucky to $29,700 in New Jersey. Professional correctional officers' salaries, overall, averaged about $22,900 and ranged from $17,000 in Wyoming to $34,100 in New York.

At the federal level, the starting salary was about $18,700 to $20,800 a year; supervisory correctional officers started at about $28,300 a year. Starting salaries were slightly higher in selected areas where prevailing local pay levels were higher. The average salary for all federal nonsupervisory correctional officers was about $31,460, for supervisors about $57,100.

Correctional officers usually are provided uniforms or a clothing allowance to purchase their own uniforms. Officers employed by the federal government and most state governments are covered by civil service systems or merit boards. Their retirement coverage entitles them to retire at age fifty after twenty years of service or at any age with twenty-five years of service. In the federal system and some states, correctional officers are represented by labor unions.

For Additional Information

Information about entrance requirements, training, and career opportunities for correctional officers at the state level may be obtained from state civil service commissions, departments of correction, or correctional institutions. Or write to:

The American Jail Association
2053 Day Road
Hagerstown, MD 21740-9795

Information on entrance requirements, training, and career opportunities for correctional officers at the federal level may be obtained from:

Federal Bureau of Prisons
National Recruitment Office
320 First Street NW, Room 460
Washington, DC 20534

International Association of Correctional Officers
1333 South Wabash, Box 53
Chicago, IL 60605

CHAPTER THREE

Careers in Firefighting

"I think patriotism is like charity—it begins at home."   HENRY JAMES

T he first fire departments consisted of neighbors who got together in times of crisis to help one another. "Bucket brigades" were formed to connect the closest sources of water to the fire. By the turn of the century, most local municipalities created their own professional fire departments.

Firefighters

Firefighters respond to a variety of emergency situations in which life, property, or the environment are at risk. Frequently, they are the first emergency response personnel to arrive at the scene of an accident, fire, flood, earthquake, or act of terrorism. Every year, fires and other emergency conditions take thousands of lives and destroy property worth billions of dollars. Firefighters help protect the public against these dangers whether they are career firefighters or volunteers who serve without pay.

Firefighting is potentially a hazardous occupation. Injuries can result from smoke inhalation, flames, and walls and floors collapsing. Exposure to hazardous materials is also a possibility even with the protective gear firefighters wear.

Most calls that firefighters respond to involve emergencies of a medical nature, and many fire departments provide ambulance service for victims. Firefighters receive training in emergency medical procedures, and many fire departments require them to be certified as emergency medical technicians.

When on duty, firefighters must always be prepared to respond immediately to a fire or other emergency situations that arise. Because firefighting is dangerous and complicated, it requires organization and teamwork. At each emergency scene, firefighters are assigned specific duties by a superior officer. These could be connecting hose lines to hydrants, positioning ladders, or operating pumps. Firefighters may rescue victims and administer emergency medical aid, ventilate smoke-filled areas, operate equipment, and salvage the contents of buildings. Their duties may change several times while the company is in action. Sometimes they remain at the site of a disaster for several days or more, rescuing survivors and assisting with medical emergencies.

A firefighter's responsibilities have become more complex in recent years due to the use of increasingly sophisticated equipment. In addition, many firefighters have assumed a wider range of responsibilities. For example, they may find themselves assisting in the recovery from natural disasters such as earthquakes and tornadoes or becoming involved with the control and cleanup of oil spills or other hazardous materials incidents.

Firefighters are primarily involved with protecting structures, but they also work at airports, at chemical plants, on crash and rescue crews, near waterfronts, and in forests and wildland areas. In forests, air patrols locate fires and report their findings to headquarters by telephone or radio. Fire rangers patrol areas of the forest to locate and report fires and hazardous conditions and to ensure that travelers and campers are complying with fire regulations. When fires break out, firefighters use hand tools and water hoses to battle the blaze. When necessary, specialized firefighters parachute from airplanes in order to reach inaccessible areas.

Most fire departments are usually headed by a fire marshal, who is in charge of the fire prevention division. Fire inspectors are specially trained to conduct inspections of structures, prevent fires, and ensure fire code compliance. They may also check and approve plans for new buildings, working with developers and planners in that process. Fire prevention personnel often speak on these subjects before public assemblies and civic organizations.

Some firefighters become fire investigators, who determine the origin and cause of fires. They collect evidence, interview witnesses, and prepare reports on fires where there may be arson or criminal negligence. Some investigators even have the power of police officers and may be allowed to arrest suspects and testify in court.

Between alarms, firefighters are required to attend classes, clean and maintain equipment, conduct practice drills and fire inspections, and participate in physical fitness activities. They prepare written reports on fire incidents and review fire science literature to keep abreast of technological developments and administrative practices and policies.

Firefighters spend much of their time at fire stations, which usually have facilities for dining and sleeping. When an alarm comes in, firefighters must respond rapidly, regardless of the weather or hour. They may spend arduous periods on their feet, sometimes in adverse weather, tending to fires, medical emergencies, hazardous-materials incidents, and other emergencies.

Firefighters often work long hours—perhaps more than fifty hours a week. In some cities, they are on duty for twenty-four hours, off for forty-eight hours, then receive an extra day off at intervals. In other cities, they work a day shift of ten hours for three or four days, a night shift of fourteen hours for three or four nights, have three or four days off, and then repeat the cycle. In addition, firefighters often work extra hours at fires and other emergencies and are regularly assigned to work on holidays. Fire lieutenants and fire captains often work the same hours as the firefighters they supervise. Shift hours include time when firefighters study, train, and perform fire-prevention duties.

Qualifications and Training

Candidates for municipal firefighting jobs may be required to pass written examinations; tests of strength, physical stamina, coordination, and agility; and a medical examination that includes drug screening. (Once on the job, workers may be monitored for drug use on a random basis.) Examinations are open to persons between eighteen and thirty-one years of age who have a high school education or the equivalent. Those who receive the highest scores and those who have completed community college courses in fire science have the best chances for appointment. In recent years, an increasing proportion of entrants to this occupation have some postsecondary education to their credit.

Usually, beginners in large fire departments are trained for several weeks at the department's training center. Through classroom instruction and practical training, the recruits study firefighting techniques, fire prevention, hazardous materials, local building codes, and emergency medical procedures, including first aid and cardiopulmonary resuscitation. Also, they learn how to use axes, saws, chemical extinguishers, ladders, and other firefighting and rescue equipment. After successfully completing this training, they are assigned to a fire company, where they undergo a period of probation.

A number of fire departments have accredited three- or four-year apprenticeship programs. These programs combine formal, technical instruction with on-the-job training under the supervision of experienced firefighters. Technical instruction covers subjects such as emergency medical procedures, firefighting techniques and equipment, fire prevention and safety, and chemical hazards associated with various combustible building materials.

To improve job performance and prepare for examinations, most experienced firefighters continue studying. Today, firefighters need more training to operate increasingly sophisticated equipment and to deal safely with the greater hazards associated with fighting fires in larger, more elaborate structures. To progress to higher-level positions, they must acquire expertise in the most advanced firefighting equipment and techniques and in building construction, emergency medical procedures, writing, public speaking, management, budgeting procedures, and labor relations. Fire departments frequently conduct training programs, and some firefighters attend training sessions sponsored by the National Fire Academy. These training sessions cover various topics, including executive development, antiarson techniques, and public fire safety and education. Some states also have extensive firefighter training programs.

Many colleges and universities offer courses leading to two- or four-year degrees in fire engineering or fire science. Many fire departments offer firefighters incentives such as tuition reimbursement or higher pay for completing advanced training.

Desirable qualities for firefighters include endurance, courage, mental alertness, a sense of public service, proficient communication skills, mechanical aptitude, and strength. Initiative and good judgment are extremely important because firefighters often must make quick decisions in emergencies. Because members of a crew eat, sleep, and work closely together under conditions of stress and danger, they should be dependable and able to get along well with others in a group. Leadership qualities are necessary for officers, who must establish and maintain discipline and efficiency as well as direct the activities of firefighters in their companies.

Opportunities for promotion are good in most fire departments. As firefighters gain experience, they may advance to higher ranks. The line of promotion usually is from firefighter to:

- engineer

- lieutenant

- captain

- battalion chief

- assistant chief

- deputy chief

- chief

Advancement generally depends upon scores on a written examination, job performance, and seniority. Increasingly, fire departments are using assessment centers which simulate a variety of actual job performance tasks to screen for the best candidates for promotion. Many fire departments now require a bachelor's degree, preferably in public administration or a related field, for promotion to positions higher than battalion chief. Some departments now require a master's degree for the chief and for executive fire officer certification from the National Fire Academy or for state chief officer certification. Firefighters stay abreast of technology and new techniques in the profession through conferences, seminars, and workshops.

Job Settings

Firefighters hold about 284,000 jobs. Nine of every ten work in municipal or county fire departments. (Some very large cities have several thousand firefighters, while many small towns have only a few.) Most of the remainder work in fire departments on federal and state installations, including airports. Private firefighting companies employ a small number.

Salaries

Median weekly earnings for firefighting occupations is about $658. The middle 50 percent earn between $513 and $832 weekly. The lowest 10 percent earn less than $387, while the highest 10 percent earn more than $979. The average annual salary for all firefighters in the federal government in nonsupervisory, supervisory, and managerial positions is about $28,800. Firefighters with five years of experience average about $32,000; those with ten years of experience average about $52,000. Fire lieutenants and fire captains may earn considerably more.

The law requires that overtime be paid to those firefighters who average fifty-three or more hours a week during a work period, which ranges from seven to twenty-eight days. Firefighters often earn overtime for working extra shifts to maintain minimum staffing levels or for special emergencies.

Practically all fire departments provide protective clothing (helmets, boots, and coats) and breathing apparatus, and many also provide dress uniforms. Firefighters generally are covered by pension plans that often provide retirement (at half pay) at age fifty after twenty-five years of service (or at any age if disabled in the line of duty).

Many career firefighters are unionized and belong to the International Association of Firefighters. Many company officers and chief officers belong to the International Association of Fire Chiefs.

For Additional Information

International Association of Fire Chiefs
4025 Fair Ridge Drive
Fairfax, VA 22033-2868

International Association of Firefighters
1750 New York Avenue NW
Washington, DC 20006

Fire Administration
16825 South Seaton Avenue
Emittsburg, MD 21727

National Fire Academy
Degrees at a Distance Program
16825 South Seton Avenue
Emmitsburg, MD 21727

Information about firefighter professional qualifications and a list of colleges and universities that offer two- or four-year degree programs in fire science or fire prevention may be obtained from:

National Fire Protection Association
1 Batterymarch Park
Quincy, MA 02269

U.S. Fire Administration
16825 South Seton Avenue
Emmitsburg, MD 21727

Emergency Medical Technicians

Sometimes firefighters may act as both emergency medical technicians (EMTs) and firefighters and sometimes they are separate entities.

Automobile accident injuries, heart attacks, near drownings, unscheduled childbirths, poisonings, and gunshot wounds all demand urgent medical attention. Emergency medical technicians (EMTs) are the ones who provide that immediate care and then transport the sick or injured to medical facilities.

Following instructions from a dispatcher, EMTs, who usually work in pairs in specially equipped vehicles, are called to emergency scenes. If necessary, they request additional help from police or fire department personnel. They determine the nature and extent of the patient's injuries or illness while also trying to determine whether the patient has epilepsy, diabetes, or other preexisting medical conditions. EMTs then give appropriate emergency care based upon the strict guidelines that dictate the procedures they may perform. All EMTs, including those with basic skills, the EMT-Basic, may open airways, restore breathing, control bleeding, treat for shock, administer oxygen, immobilize fractures, bandage wounds, assist in childbirth, manage emotionally disturbed patients, treat and assist heart attack victims, give initial care to poison and burn victims, and treat patients with antishock trousers (which prevent a person's blood pressure from falling too low).

EMT-Intermediates, or EMT-Is, have more advanced training that allows them to administer intravenous fluids, use defibrillators to give lifesaving shocks to a stopped heart, and perform other intensive care procedures.

EMT-Paramedics, EMT-Ps, provide the most extensive prehospital care. In addition to the procedures already described, paramedics may administer drugs either intravenously or orally, interpret electrocardiograms (EKGs), and use monitors and other complex equipment.

When victims are trapped, as in the case of an automobile accident, cave-in, or building collapse, EMTs free them or provide emergency care while others free them. Some conditions are simple enough to be handled by following general rules and guidelines. More complicated problems can only be carried out under the step-by-step direction of medical personnel by radio contact.

When transporting patients to a medical facility, EMTs may use special equipment, such as backboards, to immobilize the patients before placing them on stretchers and securing them in the ambulance. While one EMT drives, the other monitors the patient's vital signs and gives additional care as needed.

At a medical facility, EMTs transfer patients to the emergency department, report to the staff their observations and the care they provided, and help provide emergency treatment.

In rural areas, some EMT-Ps are trained to treat patients with minor injuries on the scene of an accident or at their homes without transporting them to a medical facility.

After each run, EMTs replace used supplies and check equipment. If patients have had a contagious disease, EMTs decontaminate the interior of the ambulance and report cases to the proper authorities.

EMTs work both indoors and outdoors, in all kinds of weather. Much of their time is spent standing, kneeling, bending, and lifting. They may risk noise-induced hearing loss from ambulance sirens and back injuries from lifting patients. EMTs may be exposed to diseases such as hepatitis B and AIDS, as well as violence from individuals suffering with drug overdoses or those who are too sick to be cognizant of their actions. Not surprisingly, the work is not only physically strenuous, but stressful.

EMTs employed by fire departments often have about a fifty-hour workweek. Those employed by hospitals frequently work between forty-five and fifty-eight hours a week, and those in private ambulance services between forty-eight and fifty-one hours. Some EMTs, especially those in police and fire departments, are on call for extended periods. Because most emergency services function twenty-four hours a day, EMTs have irregular working hours that add to job stress.

Despite the difficult working conditions, many emergency medical technicians find their work exciting and challenging.

Qualifications and Training

Formal training is needed to become an EMT. EMT-Basic training requires 100 to 120 hours of classroom work plus 10 hours of internship in a hospital emergency room. Training is available in all fifty states and in the District of Columbia and is also offered by police, fire, and health departments; in hospitals; and as a nondegree course in colleges and universities.

The EMT-Basic program provides instruction and practice in dealing with bleeding, fractures, airway obstruction, cardiac arrest, and emergency childbirth. Students learn to use and care for common emergency equipment, such as backboards, suction devices, splints, oxygen-delivery systems, and stretchers.

EMT-Intermediate training varies from state to state, but includes thirty-five to fifty-five hours of additional instruction in patient assessment as well as in the use of esophageal airways devices, intravenous fluids, and antishock garments. Training programs for EMT-Paramedics generally last between 750 and 2,000 hours. Refresher courses and continuing education are available for EMTs at all levels.

Applicants to an EMT training course generally must be at least eighteen years old and have a high school diploma (or the equivalent) and a driver's license. Recommended high school subjects for prospective EMTs are driver education, health, and science. Training in the armed forces as a "medic" is also good preparation. In addition to EMT training, EMTs in fire and police departments must be qualified as firefighters or police officers.

Graduates of approved EMT-Basic training programs who pass a written and practical examination administered by the state certifying agency or the National Registry of Emergency Medical Technicians earn the title of Registered EMT-Basic. Prerequisites for taking the EMT-Intermediate examination include registration as an EMT-Basic, required classroom work, and a specified amount of clinical experience and field internship. Registration for EMT-Paramedics by the National Registry of Emergency Medical Technicians or a state emergency medical services agency requires current registration or state certification as an EMT-Basic, completion of an EMT-Paramedic training program and required clinical and field internships, as well as passing a written and practical examination. Although not a general requirement for employment, registration acknowledges an EMTs qualifications and makes higher-paying jobs easier to obtain.

All fifty states have some kind of certification procedure. In thirty-one states and the District of Columbia, registration with the national registry is required at some or all levels of certification. Other states require their own certification examinations or provide the option of taking the national registry examination.

To maintain their certification, all EMTs must reregister, usually every two years. In order to reregister, an individual must be working as an EMT and meet a continuing education requirement.

EMTs should be emotionally stable, have good dexterity, agility, and coordination, and be able to lift and carry heavy loads. EMTs need good eyesight (corrective lenses may be used) with accurate color vision.

Advancement beyond the EMT-Paramedic level usually means leaving fieldwork. An EMT-Paramedic can become a supervisor, operations manager, administrative director, or executive director of emergency services. Some EMTs become EMT instructors, firefighters, dispatchers, or police officers; others move into sales or marketing of emergency medical equipment. Finally, some become EMTs to assess their interest in health care and then decide to return to school to become registered nurses, physicians, or other health workers.

Job Settings

There are about 138,000 EMTs in the United States. Two-fifths serve in private ambulance services; about a third are in municipal fire, police, or rescue squad departments; and a quarter serve in hospitals. In addition, there are many volunteer EMTs. Most career EMTs work in metropolitan areas. Smaller towns often don't have the funds to employ EMTs.

Salaries

Earnings of EMTs depend on the employment setting and geographic location as well as the individual's training and experience. According to a recent survey conducted by the *Journal of Emergency Medical Services*, average starting salaries are $19,919 for EMT-Ambulance or EMT-Basic, $21,818 for EMT-Intermediate, and $23,861 for EMT-Paramedic.

EMTs working in fire departments average the highest annual salaries of emergency medical technicians: figures range from $26,000 to $31,000 for all employers, $22,000 to $28,000 for private ambulance services, $22,000 to $29,000 for hospitals, and $28,000 to $37,000 for fire departments.

Those in emergency medical services that are part of fire or police departments receive the same benefits as firefighters or police officers.

For Additional Information

Information concerning training courses, registration, and job opportunities for EMTs can be obtained by writing to the state director of emergency medical services. General information about EMTs is available from:

National Association of Emergency Medical Technicians
102 West Leake Street
Clinton, MS 39056

National Registry of Emergency Medical Technicians
P.O. Box 29233
Columbus, OH 43229

CHAPTER FOUR

Careers in the Military

"I only regret that I have but one life to lose for my country." NATHAN HALE

For many, the lure of serving one's country and seeing the world is best fulfilled by spending time in the military. And luckily this is the case, because in order to maintain a strong national defense, a vast number of individuals performing diverse jobs are needed. These include (among others) people managing hospitals, individuals commanding tank crews, technical personnel programming computers, professionals operating nuclear reactors, and specialists repairing and maintaining helicopters. The military's occupational diversity provides educational opportunities and work experience in literally hundreds of occupations for those willing to make the commitment to their country.

The Military Branches

The United States Air Force, Air Force Reserve, and Air National Guard defend the United States by controlling air and space. Stationed all over the world, they fly and maintain aircraft, missiles, and spacecraft.

The United States Army, Army Reserve, and Army National Guard protect and defend the United States and its interests by maintaining ground troops, tanks, helicopters, and missile systems. They may be involved in land-based operations all over the world.

The United States Coast Guard and Coast Guard Reserve serve as a branch of the armed services and as a service within the United States Department of Transportation. They act as the main maritime law enforcement agency for the United States.

The United States Marine Corps and Marine Corps Reserve combine to form an elite fighting force that operates within the Department of the Navy. Marines guard United States embassies, protect naval bases, serve on ships, and remain ready at a moment's notice to protect the interests of the United States anywhere in the world.

The United States Navy and Navy Reserve defend the United States and its allies, providing clear access to travel throughout the world's oceans. Navy personnel may serve on submarines, on ships, at bases on shore, and in aviation positions in any part of the world.

Military Personnel

Military personnel hold a myriad of managerial and administrative jobs; professional, technical, and clerical jobs; construction jobs; electrical and electronics jobs; mechanical and repair jobs; and many others. The military provides training and work experience for people who serve a single enlistment of three to six years of active duty, for those who embark on a career that lasts twenty years or more, and for those who serve in the Army, Navy, Marine, Air Force, and Coast Guard Reserves and Army and Air National Guard.

There are more than 360 basic and advanced military occupational specialties for enlisted personnel and almost as many for officers. More than 75 percent of these occupational specialties have civilian counterparts.

The front line of the armed forces consists of infantry, gun crews, and seamanship specialists. Officers plan and direct military operations, oversee security activities, and serve as combat leaders and pilots. Enlisted personnel serve as infantry or weapons specialists; aircraft crew members; armored and amphibious vehicle crew; artillery, gunnery, or rocket specialists; and combat engineers. Some of these specialties involve skills that can be applied to a number of civilian occupations, such as police officers, commercial pilots, and heavy-equipment operators. In addition, people in this category learn how to work as team members and develop leadership, managerial, and supervisory skills.

Military personnel assigned to electronic equipment repair occupations are responsible for maintaining and repairing many different types of equipment.

Officers oversee the regular maintenance and repair of avionics, communications, radar, and air traffic control equipment. Enlisted personnel repair radio, navigation, missile guidance, and flight control equipment as well as telephone and data processing equipment. Many of these skills are directly transferable to jobs in the civilian sector.

Communications and intelligence specialists in the military have civilian scientific, engineering, and investigative counterparts. Officers serve as intelligence gatherers and interpreters, cryptologists, information analysts, translators, and in related intelligence occupations. Enlisted personnel work as computer programmers; air traffic controllers; interpreters and translators; radio, radar, and sonar operators; and interrogation and investigative specialists.

Military medical and dental occupations all have civilian counterparts. Physicians, dentists, optometrists, nurses, therapists, veterinarians, pharmacists, and others in health diagnostic and treatment occupations hold the rank of health-care officers.

Enlisted personnel are trained to work as medical laboratory technologists and technicians, radiological technologists, emergency medical technicians, dental assistants, optical assistants, pharmaceutical assistants, sanitation specialists, and veterinary assistants. Training for health professionals that is obtained in the military is usually recognized in the civilian sector and service-trained health professionals are eligible to apply for certification or registration, which is often a hiring prerequisite.

Military experience in other technical and allied specialty occupations is often directly transferable to civilian life. Officers in this field work as meteorologists, mapping directors, television and motion picture directors, and band directors. Enlisted personnel are trained to work as photographers, motion picture camera operators, mapping and surveying specialists, illustrators, weather data collectors, explosives disposal specialists, divers, and musicians.

Functional support and administrative occupations in military service require the same skills as similar jobs in the private sector and government agencies. Officers in this category work as directors, executives, adjutants, administrative officers, personnel managers, training administrators, budget officers, financial officers, public affairs officers, accountants, hospital administrators, inspectors, computer systems managers, and lawyers. Enlisted personnel in this category work as accounting, payroll, personnel, and postal clerks; computer programmers and operators; chaplain assistants; counseling aides; typists; and storekeepers.

Those in electrical and mechanical equipment repair occupations maintain aircraft, motor vehicles, and ships. Officers oversee maintenance of aircraft, missiles, conventional and nuclear-powered ships, trucks, earth-moving equipment, and other vehicles. Enlisted personnel serve as mechanics, engine specialists, and boiler technicians. They also install and maintain wire communications systems such as telephones. Skills obtained in these jobs are readily transferable to those in the civilian sector.

Military personnel assigned to craft occupations are considered skilled craftspeople. Officers serve as civil engineers and architects and manage the work of enlisted personnel who work as carpenters, construction equipment operators, metalworkers, machinists, plumbers, welders, electricians, and heating and air-conditioning specialists.

Military personnel in service and supply occupations handle food service, security, and personal services and supply. Officers work as logistics officers, supply managers, transportation and traffic managers, and procurement officers.

Enlisted personnel include military police, correctional specialists, criminal investigators, firefighters, and food preparation and other service workers. They operate or service transportation equipment, such as trucks, ships, boats, airplanes, and helicopters, and act as quartermasters, supply specialists, and cargo specialists. Many of these skills can be transferred to civilian occupations.

Working Conditions

Military life is much more regimented than civilian life, and one must be willing to accept the discipline. It is important to remember that signing an enlistment contract obligates you to serve for a specified period of time.

Dress and grooming requirements are stringent, and rigid formalities govern many aspects of everyday life. For instance, officers and enlisted personnel do not socialize together, and commissioned officers are saluted and addressed as "sir" or "ma'am." These and other rules encourage respect for superiors whose commands must be obeyed immediately and without question.

The needs of the military always come first. As a result, hours and working conditions can vary substantially. However, most military personnel not deployed on a mission usually work eight hours a day, five days a week. While off duty, military personnel usually do not wear their uniforms and are free to participate in family and recreational activities like most civilians. Some assignments, however, require night and weekend work or require people to be on call at all hours. All assignments may require substantial travel. Depending on the service, assignments may require long periods at sea, sometimes in cramped quarters or lengthy overseas assignments in countries offering few amenities. Some individuals serve tours in isolated parts of the world where they are subject to extreme cold or heat and the possibility of hostilities breaking out at any time. Others, such as sailors on carrier flight deck duty, have jobs that are hazardous even in noncombat situations.

During wartime, many military personnel engage in combat and find themselves in life or death situations. They rely on countless hours of training to produce teamwork that is critical to the success or failure of an operation and to protecting the lives of the individuals in their units. Rapidly advancing military technology has made warfare more precise and lethal, further increasing the need for teamwork. Noncombatants may also face danger if their duties bring them close to a combat zone. Even in peacetime, most members of the combat arms branches of the military participate in hazardous training activities.

Ship and air crews travel extensively, while others in the military are stationed at bases throughout the country or overseas. Military personnel are usually transferred to a new duty station every few years. Satisfactory job performance generally assures steady employment and earnings, and many necessities—such as meals, clothing, and living quarters—are provided.

Qualifications and Training

As it has since 1973, the military expects to meet its personnel requirements through volunteers. Enlisted members must enter a legal agreement called an enlistment contract, which usually involves a commitment to eight years of service. Depending on the terms of the contract, two to six years are spent on active duty, the balance in the reserves. The enlistment contract obligates the service to provide the agreed-upon options—job, rating, pay, cash bonuses for enlistment in certain occupations, medical and other benefits, occupational training, and continuing education. In return, enlisted personnel must serve satisfactorily for the specified period of time.

Requirements for each service vary, but certain qualifications for enlistment are common to all branches. An enlistee must be between the ages of seventeen and thirty-five, must be a United States citizen or immigrant alien holding permanent resident status, must not have a felony record, and must possess a birth certificate. Applicants who are seventeen must have the consent of a parent or legal guardian before entering the service. Air force enlisted personnel must enter active duty before age twenty-eight.

Applicants must pass both a written examination—the Armed Services Vocational Aptitude Battery—and meet certain minimum physical standards, such as height, weight, vision, and overall health. All branches prefer high school graduation or its equivalent and require it for certain enlistment options. In 1997, more than 90 percent of enlistees were high school graduates. Single parents are generally not eligible to enlist.

People thinking about enlisting in the military should learn as much as they can about military life before making a decision. This is especially important if you are thinking about making the military a career. Speaking to friends and relatives with military experience is a good idea. Determine what the military can offer you and what it will expect in return. Then talk to a recruiter, who can determine if you qualify for enlistment, can explain the various enlistment options, and can tell you which military occupational specialties currently have openings for trainees. Bear in mind that the recruiter's job is to recruit promising applicants into the military, so the information he or she gives you is likely to stress the positive aspects of military life.

Ask the recruiter to assess your chances of being accepted for training in the occupation or occupations of your choice or, better still, take the aptitude exam to see how well you score. The military uses the aptitude exam as a placement exam, and test scores largely determine an individual's chances of being accepted into a particular training program.

Selection for a particular type of training depends on the needs of the service, general and technical aptitudes, and personal preference. Because all prospective recruits are required to take the exam, those who do so before committing themselves to enlist have the advantage of knowing in advance whether they stand a good chance of being accepted for training in a particular specialty.

The recruiter can schedule you for the Armed Services Vocational Aptitude Battery without any obligation. Many high schools offer the exam as an easy way for students to explore the possibility of a military career, and the test also provides insight into career areas where the student has demonstrated aptitudes and interests.

The Armed Forces Process

Enlistment Contract

If you decide to join the military, the next step is to pass the physical examination and then enter into the enlistment contract. This involves choosing, qualifying, and agreeing on a number of enlistment options such as length of active-duty time, which may vary according to the enlistment option. (Most active-duty programs have enlistment options ranging from three to six years, although there are some two-year programs.) The contract will also state the date of enlistment and other options, such as bonuses and types of training to be received. If the service is unable to fulfill its part of the contract (such as providing a certain kind of training), the contract may become null and void.

All services offer a "delayed-entry program" by which an enlistee can delay entry into active duty for up to one year. High school students can enlist during senior year and enter a branch of military service after graduation. Others choose this program because the job training they desire is not currently available but will be within the coming year or because they need time to arrange personal affairs.

Women are eligible to enter almost all military specialties. Although many women serve in medical and administrative support positions, women also work as mechanics, missile maintenance technicians, heavy-equipment operators, fighter pilots, and intelligence officers. Only occupations involving a high probability of direct exposure to combat are excluded—for example, the artillery and infantry branches of the army.

People planning to apply the skills gained through military training to a civilian career should look into several things before selecting a military occupation. First, they should determine how good the prospects are for civilian employment in jobs related to the military specialty that interests them. Second, they should know the prerequisites for the related civilian job. Many occupations require a license, certification, or a minimum level of education. In such cases, it is important to determine whether military training is sufficient to enter the civilian equivalent or, if not, what additional training will be required.

Training Programs for Enlisted Personnel
Following enlistment, new members of the armed forces undergo recruit training. Better known as "basic" training, recruit

training provides a six- to eleven-week introduction to military life with courses in health, first aid, and military skills and protocol. Days and nights are carefully structured and include rigorous physical exercises designed to improve strength and endurance.

Following basic training, most recruits take additional training at technical schools that prepare them for a particular military occupational specialty. The formal training period generally lasts from ten to twenty weeks, although training for certain occupations—nuclear power plant operator, for example—may take as much as one year. Recruits not assigned to classroom instruction receive on-the-job training at the first duty assignment.

Many service people get college credit for the technical training they receive on duty, which, combined with off-duty courses, can lead to an associate's degree through community college programs such as the Community College of the Air Force.

In addition to on-duty training, military personnel may choose from a variety of educational programs. Most military installations have tuition-assistance programs for people wishing to take courses during off-duty hours. These may be correspondence courses or degree programs offered by local colleges or universities. Tuition assistance pays up to 75 percent of college costs.

Also available are courses designed to help service personnel earn high school equivalency diplomas. Each service branch provides opportunities for full-time study to a limited number of exceptional applicants. Military personnel accepted into these highly competitive programs receive full pay, allowances, tuition, and related fees. In return, they must agree to serve an additional amount of time in the service. Other very selective programs enable enlisted personnel to qualify as commissioned officers through additional military training.

Officer Training

Officer training in the armed forces is provided through the federal service academies (military, naval, air force, and Coast Guard); the Reserve Officers' Training Corps (ROTC); Officer Candidate School (OCS) or Officer Training School (OTS); the National Guard (State Officer Candidate School programs); the Uniformed Services University of Health Sciences; and other programs. All are very selective and are good options for those wishing to make the military a career.

Federal service academies provide a four-year college program leading to a bachelor of science degree. The midshipman or cadet is provided free room and board, tuition, medical care, and a monthly allowance. Graduates receive regular or reserve commissions and have a five-year active-duty obligation, or longer if entering flight training.

To become a candidate for appointment as a cadet or midshipman in one of the service academies, most applicants obtain a nomination from an authorized source (usually a member of Congress). Candidates do not need to know a member of Congress personally to request a nomination. Nominees must have an academic record of the requisite quality, college aptitude test scores above an established minimum, and recommendations from teachers or school officials. They must also pass a medical examination. Appointments are then made from the list of eligible nominees.

Appointments to the Coast Guard Academy are made strictly on a competitive basis. A nomination is not required.

ROTC programs train students in about 950 Army, 60 Navy and Marine Corps, and 550 Air Force units at participating colleges and universities. Trainees take two to five hours of military instruction a week in addition to regular college courses.

After graduation, they may serve as officers on active duty for a stipulated period of time, at the convenience of the service.

Some may serve their obligations in the National Reserves or Guard. In the last two years of an ROTC program, students receive a monthly allowance while attending school and additional pay for summer training. ROTC scholarships for two, three, and four years are available on a competitive basis.

All scholarships pay for tuition and have allowances for subsistence, textbooks, supplies, and other fees. College graduates can earn a commission in the armed forces through OCS or OTS programs in the U.S. Army, Navy, Air Force, Marine Corps, Coast Guard, and National Guard. These officers must serve their obligations on active duty.

Those with training in certain health professions may qualify for direct appointment as officers. In the case of health professions students, financial assistance and internship opportunities are available from the military in return for specified periods of military service. For example, prospective medical students can apply to the Uniformed Services University of Health Sciences, which offers free tuition in a program leading to an M.D. degree. In return, graduates must serve for seven years in either the military or the Public Health Service. Direct appointments also are available for those qualified to serve in other special duties, such as the judge advocate general (legal) or chaplain corps.

Flight training is available to commissioned officers in each branch of the armed forces. In addition, the army has a direct enlistment option to become a warrant officer aviator.

Advancement Opportunities

Each service has different criteria for promoting personnel. Generally, the first few promotions for both enlisted and officer personnel come easily; subsequent promotions are much more competitive.

Criteria for promotion may include time in service and grade, job performance, a fitness report (supervisor's recommendation), and written examinations. People who are passed over for promotion several times generally must leave the military.

Salaries

Most enlisted personnel start as recruits at Grade E-1. However, those with special skills or above-average education may start as high as Grade E-4. Most warrant officers start at Grade W-1 or W-2, depending upon their occupational and academic qualifications and their branch of service. Most commissioned officers start at Grade O-1; highly trained officers—for example, physicians, engineers, and scientists—may start as high as Grade O-3 or O-4.

The following lists show military basic pay by grade for active duty personnel with fewer than two years service at grade, as of 1997.

Army

Commissioned Officers	Monthly Pay
O-6 Colonel	$3,638.40
O-5 Lieutenant Colonel	$2,910.30
O-4 Major	$2,452.80
O-3 Captain	$2,279.40
O-2 lst Lieutenant	$1,987.80
O-1 2nd Lieutenant	$1,725.90
Warrant Officers	
W-2 Chief Warrant Officer	$1,848.60
W-1 Warrant Officer	$1,540.20

Enlisted Personnel	Monthly Pay
E-6 Staff Sergeant	$1,360.80
E-5 Sergeant	$1,194.30
E-4 Corporal/Specialist	$1,113.60
E-3 Private First Class	$1,049.70
E-2 Private	$1,010.10
E-1 Private	$900.90

Navy and Coast Guard

Officers	Monthly Pay
O-6 Captain	$3,638.40
O-5 Commander	$2,910.30
O-4 Lieutenant Commander	$2,452.80
O-3 Lieutenant	$2,279.40
O-2 Lieutenant (JG)	$1,987.80
O-1 Ensign	$1,725.90
Warrant Officers	
W-2 Chief Warrant Officer	$1,848.60
W-1 Warrant Officer	$1,540.20
Enlisted Personnel	
E-6 Petty Officer list Class	$1,360.80
E-5 Petty Officer 2nd Class	$1,194.30
E-4 Petty Officer 3rd Class	$1,113.60
E-3 Seaman	$1,049.70
E-2 Seaman Apprentice	$1,010.10
E-1 Seaman Recruit	$900.90

Air Force

Officers	Monthly Pay
O-6 Colonel	$3,638.40
O-5 Lieutenant Colonel	$2,910.30
O-4 Major	$2,452.80
O-3 Captain	$2,279.40
O-2 First Lieutenant	$1,987.80
O-1 Second Lieutenant	$1,725.90
Enlisted Personnel	
E-6 Technical Sergeant	$1,360.80
E-5 Staff Sergeant	$1,194.30
E-4 Senior Airman	$1,113.60
E-3 Airman First Class	$1,049.70
E-2 Airman	$1,010.10
E-1 Airman Basic	$900.90

Marine Corps

Officers	Monthly Pay
O-6 Colonel	$3,638.40
O-5 Lieutenant Colonel	$2,910.30
O-4 Major	$2,452.80
O-3 Captain	$2,279.40
O-2 First Lieutenant	$1,987.80
O-1 Second Lieutenant	$1,725.90
Warrant Officers	
W-2 Chief Warrant Officer	$1,848.60
W-1 Warrant Officer	$1,540.20

Enlisted Personnel	Monthly Pay
E-6 Staff Sergeant	$1,360.80
E-5 Sergeant	$1,194.30
E-4 Corporal	$1,113.60
E-3 Lance Corporal	$1,049.70
E-2 Private First Class	$1,010.10
E-1 Private	$900.90

Allowances

In addition to basic pay, military personnel receive free room and board (or a tax-free housing and subsistence allowance), medical and dental care, a military clothing allowance, military supermarket and department store shopping privileges, thirty days of paid vacation a year (referred to as leave), and travel opportunities. Other allowances are paid for foreign duty, hazardous duty, submarine and flight duty, and employment as a medical officer.

A variety of educational programs for undergraduate and graduate degrees are possible, including tuition assistance for programs at colleges and universities.

Qualified veterans may be able to receive a guaranteed home loan with no money down as part of the Department of Veterans Affairs Home Loan Guarantee Program.

Athletic and other recreational facilities—such as libraries, gymnasiums, tennis courts, golf courses, bowling centers, and movies—are available on many military installations.

Military personnel are eligible for retirement benefits after twenty years of service. This provides an opportunity for a second career with a second source of retirement income. Those who retire with more than twenty years of military service receive higher pay. In addition, individuals receive medical care and commissary/exchange privileges. National Guard personnel and reservists may also earn twenty-year retirements. However, the payment formula is based upon the fact that the duty was part-time.

Veterans' Benefits

The Veterans Administration (VA) provides numerous benefits to those who have served at least two years in the armed forces. Veterans are eligible for free care in VA hospitals for all service-connected disabilities regardless of time served; those with other medical problems are eligible for free VA care if they are unable to pay the cost of hospitalization elsewhere. Admission to a VA medical center depends on the availability of beds, however.

Veterans are also eligible for certain loans, including home loans. Veterans, regardless of health, can convert a military life-insurance policy to an individual policy with any participating company in the veteran's state of residence. In addition, job counseling, testing, and placement services are available.

Veterans who participate in the New Montgomery GI Bill Program receive educational benefits. Under this program, armed forces personnel may elect to deduct from their pay up to $100 a month to put toward future education for the first twelve months of active duty. Veterans who serve on active duty for three years or more, or two years active duty plus four years in the Selected Reserve or National Guard, will receive $427.87 a month in basic benefits for thirty-six months. Those who enlist and serve for less than three years will receive $347.65 a month. In addition, each service provides its own additional contributions to put toward future education. This sum becomes the service member's educational fund. Upon separation from active duty, the fund can be used to finance an education at any VA-approved institution. VA-approved schools include many vocational, correspondence, business, technical, and flight training schools; community and junior colleges; and colleges and universities.

Information on educational and other veterans' benefits is available from VA offices located throughout the country.

Meet Lise Hull, Oceansystems Watch Officer

Lise Hull earned a bachelor of arts degree in anthropology from Franklin and Marshall College in Lancaster, Pennsylvania, in 1976 and a master's degree in management of public affairs (specializing in historic preservation) from Indiana University in Bloomington in 1981. In addition, she holds a master of arts degree (with distinction) in counseling psychology from National University, Sacramento, California.

"I was attracted to the navy by the opportunity to have a lengthy career path and, even more so, to have the chance to see the world," says Hull. "I was bored with my job at the time and wanted something that would offer more to me. I saw an ad in the newspaper, and decided to 'go for it.' I had a talk with a counselor at Officer Candidate School (OCS) who had been an Oceansystems Watch Officer (OWO). She talked about how fascinating the work could be in that field and that there were plenty of opportunities to travel. That seemed to be an ideal choice for me!

"I joined in 1983 and became commissioned in February of 1984. I then attended Officer Candidate School in Newport, Rhode Island. I also took some additional training courses, including Oceansystems Watch Officer training, CMS Custodian training, and several classes for alcohol and drug counselors.

"During my time in the Navy, I've held several positions; one of note was as General Unrestricted Line Officer (a commissioned officer)," continues Hull. "I also worked as an oceansystems watch officer, communications officer, and director of a counseling and assistance center.

"For as long as I can remember, I have been interested in seeing the world. As a child and teenager, I did a lot of traveling with my parents and always enjoyed just observing and absorbing my surroundings. As I got older, I realized that I wanted to experience as much of the world as possible. The navy certainly offered that possibility.

"As an OWO, I work rotating shifts. A 2-2-2-80 rotation is very grueling—two eight-hour shifts from about 7 A.M. to 3 P.M., followed by two eight-hour shifts from 11 P.M. to 7 A.M. (actually, we often had to wait until after 9 A.M. to leave because we were responsible for giving the morning briefing to the commanding officer), and then two eight-hour shifts from 3 P.M. to 11 P.M. After the second day watch, unless something exciting was happening, the shifts blurred together, and on the midwatches, it was really tough trying to stay alert. Some watches were busy, others less so. So, we would do drills to keep the sailors prepared for any emergency. Those drills were fun. Some watches were more casual, and the division could relax and talk with each other, while still monitoring their work. Others were very intensive, with no time for joking.

"The things I liked about that particular job were the friendships that were formed. Sailors could transfer from facility to facility and always find familiar faces. On watch, the sections became fairly tight, like a large family. Solid friendships were formed. The work itself could be tedious, but the type of work was fascinating. But, for me, the ability to be in new places and to travel around the countryside on my days off was the obvious highlight. I got to see Alaska, Great Britain, and California—all places I had never been to before. And now I am living in Oregon, which I doubt I would be doing if I had not joined the navy. Also, the pay is great for officers, especially single officers. I could save lots of money, go anywhere, buy pretty much what I want without worrying (but that's not the case for enlisted people).

"Of course, there are downsides too—long days, difficult conditions, restrictions, and expectations. And, as an officer, you have to give the appearance of always being in control and not having any personal problems.

"It's important to know that you lose a lot of freedom in the military. You cannot be an individualist and survive. But if you want a career that takes you places and gives you lots of responsibility, this is a great opportunity. However, be sure that you can conform, that you don't mind working long hours, and that you can keep your opinions to yourself. For me, it's a great way to experience the world and other cultures and personalities. I would advise others to make the most of such opportunities. Explore those locations while you have the chance. You can experience places most people will never have the chance to."

Meet Christian R. Shaw, Police Officer and Veteran

Christian R. Shaw attended the Naval Training Center in San Diego, California, in 1985; the Federal Law Enforcement Training Center (FLETC) in Glynco, Georgia, in 1990; the U.S. Navy Fleet Training Center, Small Arms Institute, in San Diego, California, in 1993; and the Veterans Administration Law Enforcement Training Center in Little Rock, Arkansas, in 1993. Then he earned an associate's degree in adminstering to justice and subsequently attended the Los Angeles Police Academy in 1996.

"It all started in 1981, when I joined my high school Junior ROTC," Shaw says. "Then in 1985, I joined the navy with an eight-year reserve enlistment. My naval helicopter experiences during that time included the following assignments: HH-1K helicopter plane captain, United States Navy NAS Point Mugu, California, 1986; aviation shipboard (aircraft carrier) firefighting, U.S. Navy San Diego, California, 1987; HH-1K helicopter utility crewman/door bunner, U.S. Navy NAS Point Mugu, California, 1987; HH-60H helicopter plane captain, U.S. Navy NAS Point Mugu, California, 1989; HH-60H helicopter utility crewman/door gunner, U.S. Navy NAS Point Mugu, California, 1989; HH-60H helicopter crew chief, U.S. Navy NAS Point Mugu, California, 1991; and UH-60A helicopter crew chief, U.S. Army AFRC, Los Alamitos, California, in 1993.

"I also served in the United States Army National Guard in California, in the private patrol for 'Bel-Air Patrol' in California (formed by Howard Hughes), acquired and operated a small private security patrol company, and was employed by the United States Department of Justice as a correctional officer," says Shaw.

"Today I spend my days patrolling the streets of Los Angeles in a black-and-white police vehicle as a Los Angeles police officer. And part-time, on my off days, I fly for the California Army National Guard in a UH-60 Blackhawk helicopter as a helicopter crew chief (also known as a flight engineer). Flying is hard work, but I love it. It's relaxing to me.

"For the LAPD, my best moments occur when there are thanks from the citizens in the community. It's encouraging to know that you got a 'bad guy' off the street—so that he or she can't hurt anyone—at least for a while.

"As a police officer, my least favorite things are the overtime, having to go to court on off days and losing a battle I feel should have been won in court. The best part of being in the army is the people you work with and the fun war stories you share. However, there are long hours and you often have to put up with difficult living conditions."

Meet David Winstead, Veteran

David Winstead did his basic military training at Lackland Air Force Base in Texas in December of 1968. He received his technical training at Keesler Air Force Base in Mississippi in 1969 and secured his security police (law enforcement) training in

1975 at Davis Monthan Air Force Base in Arizona. In 1987, Winstead attended the Command Noncommissioned Officer Academy in Kadena Air Force Base in Japan and took an Advanced Nuclear Weapons Orientation Course at Kirtland Air Force Base in New Mexico in 1989.

"I went into the air force right out of high school in 1989," he explains. "It was during the Vietnam conflict, and it was either join or get drafted. If you joined, you could choose your career and assignment. If you were drafted, you didn't have that choice. Still, the only real reason that I joined was that I felt it was my patriotic duty. While in the military service, I found the pluses to be a steady income, rapid advancement, the opportunity to see all of Asia, the chance to make a lot of new friends, and the fact that I had thirty days of leave a year.

"I've had many titles during my tenure in the military," Winstead says. "Among them are base document security NCO (top secret control officer for the base) and security police law enforcement specialist.

"The minuses were the long hours, the necessity for strict adherence to following orders, and the fact that it was difficult on my family.

"In one sense, it was a great time, but it was also filled with destruction and horror. I would tell others who are considering military service to be sure that this is what you want. Remember that you need to be willing to give your life for your country because you never know when you might be asked to do just that."

For Additional Information

Each of the military services publishes handbooks, fact sheets, and pamphlets describing entrance requirements, training and advancement opportunities, and other aspects of military careers. These publications are widely available at all recruiting stations, most state employment service offices, and in high schools, colleges, and public libraries.

Check your local phone book for information on regional offices.

Main Recruiting Phone Numbers and Websites

United States Department of Defense
http://www.defenselink.mil

United States Army
1-800-USA-ARMY
http://www.goarmy.com

Military Academy, West Point
1-800-USA-Army
http://www.usma.edu

Army ROTC (AROTC)
1-800-USA-ROTC

Army Reserve
1-800-USA-ARMY

Army National Guard
1-800-638-7600

United States Air Force
1-800-423-USAF
http://www.af.mil

U.S. Air Force Academy, Colorado Springs
1-800-443-9266
http://www.usafa.af.mil

Air Force ROTC (AFROTC)
1-800-522-0033

Air Force Reserve
1-800-257-1212

Air National Guard
1-800-423-USAF

United States Coast Guard
1-800-GET-USCG
http://www.uscg.mil

U.S. Coast Guard Academy, New London
1-800-GET-USCG
http://www.gca.edu

Coast Guard Reserve
1-800-GET-USCG

United States Marine Corps
1-800-MARINES
http://www.usmc.mil

Marine Corps Reserve
1-800-MARINES

United States Navy
1-800-327-NAVY
http://www.navyjobs.com

U.S. Naval Academy/Annapolis
1-800-638-9156
http://www.nadn.navy.mil

Navy ROTC (NROTC)
1-800-NAV-ROTC

Navy Reserve
1-800-USA-USNR

CHAPTER FIVE

Careers in the Peace Corps

"A man's feet should be planted in his country, but his eyes should survey the world." GEORGE SANTAYANA

On March 1, 1961, at a time when the Cold War between East and West raged and Germany stood divided, President Kennedy launched the Peace Corps. In the thirty plus years since then, Peace Corps volunteers have maintained the same mission: providing volunteers to battle disease, poverty, hunger, and deprivation all over the globe and to teach people of other nations about America and Americans in order to promote world understanding. Since then, more than 140,000 Americans have served as Peace Corps volunteers. Today, 6,000 such individuals are performing their services in more than ninety countries in Asia, the Middle East, South and Central America, the Caribbean, the Pacific, Africa, and central Europe.

Peace Corps Volunteers

Host countries make specific requests for individuals with particular expertise. Some of the skills most often requested include aid in the areas of technical education, primary and secondary education, health and nutrition, natural resources, and agriculture. Volunteers are not asked simply to go over to these countries and do all the work. Their role is to serve as teacher or trainer by providing the necessary information, techniques, and expertise to the host country members so that they may perform these tasks on their own.

Qualifications and Training

Applicants for the Peace Corps must be United States citizens who are at least eighteen years old (no limit on the upper end) and healthy, free from financial debt, and willing to undergo an eight- to twelve-week training program in addition to a two-year service period. Additionally, workshops are held to reinforce skills and formulate and disseminate plans. Married couples without children are eligible as long as they meet all qualifications. It usually takes about ten months from the receipt of an application to the beginning of training. While you are able to indicate an area or areas you would like to go to, this limits your possibilities for placement.

Most assignments require a minimum of a bachelor's degree. In some cases, an associate's degree along with a specified number of years of experience may suffice. Other jobs require a master's degree or three to five years of experience in lieu of or in addition to a college degree.

Volunteers receive transportation to and from their assignment locations and twenty-four days of vacation each year. Free medical and dental care are provided along with a monthly stipend to allow for housing, food, clothes, and other living expenses. Often student loan payments are deferred for the time period of the service. Upon fulfilling the service, volunteers are given a readjustment allowance of approximately $5,400 in addition to being aided in their search for a job. Some opt to take advantage of the available eligibility for federal employment on a noncompetitive basis. Also, many institutions offer special scholarships and assistantships for volunteers who return home.

Returning volunteers cite the following benefits of Peace Corps work: a way to see diverse parts of the world, an opportunity to get to know and be of help to people in Third World countries, a rewarding feeling, and, in many cases, substantial personal growth.

Meet Kathleen Klug, Peace Corps Volunteer

Kathleen Klug learned about the Peace Corps through various social studies classes in high school. She had also developed an interest in other cultures and community service—interests that can be easily pursued in the Peace Corps. "I attended Peace Corps recruiting presentations at my university to obtain more specific information about becoming a volunteer," she says. "In the fall of my senior year, I submitted the lengthy Peace Corps application and interviewed with a recruiter. Speaking with the recruiter gave me a truer picture of the application process. I was told that it probably would be difficult to find a placement for me due to my nontechnical background. At that time (and now too), the Peace Corps tried to recruit individuals with degrees or a background in subjects such as medicine, farming, horticulture, engineering, construction, physics/chemistry/math, Teaching English as a Second Language (TESL), and so forth. However, some of my course work and volunteer experience helped me to pass this first step of the application process. (I graduated with a B.S. in psychology and political science. I also had my CPR/First Aid certification and some health education course work.)

"After my interview, I kept in regular contact with my recruiter and waited three to four months until I received a nomination (second step) in the health nutrition extension. At that time, I needed to complete information for a background check (including fingerprinting) and have a complete medical exam. In either late April or early May, I finally received an invitation (third step) to serve as water/sanitation health educator in Ghana, West Africa.

"The whole process took about eight months from the time I applied until the time I left for Ghana in July. I knew some individuals who either because of luck and/or a technical background completed the entire process in one month. The recruiting process may boil down to a certain country needing a particular type of skilled volunteer and a Peace Corps applicant having those skills *and* being available at that time.

"I completed a five-day staging (fourth step) in Chicago with the other trainees going to Ghana. The individuals in my training group were in their twenties and thirties, for the most part, and came from all over the United States. Staging is basically a time for people to get to know one another, gain general information about the Peace Corps, Ghana, etc. Then I traveled with these fifty other trainees to Ghana for our ten-week training (fifth step).

"In the beginning of July, I began training at Mfantsipim Senior Secondary School in Cape Coast, Ghana. The intensive ten weeks included training in language (Fante and Twi), culture, and technical education, in addition to field experience. During the technical phase of the training, our group was divided into sections: education, water/sanitation health education, forestry, and business, depending on an individual's assignment. In my water/sanitation health education section, I learned such things as latrine and well construction, health education (oral dehydration salts, waterborne diseases, etc.), and nonformal education methods.

"In September, I was happily sworn in as a U.S. Peace Corps Volunteer with approximately forty-six other new volunteers. I was assigned to a site in the Kumasi region of the country in a medium-size village called Manso Nkwanta (the district capital). During the first few months of my service at the site, I spent most of my time meeting with people in my village and surrounding district villages and discussing/evaluating the water sanitation health education needs. We also discussed our plans to meet these needs and how I could help facilitate these plans.

"As a health educator, I reported to a fifteen-person Manso Nkwanta District Health and Sanitation Committee, the Ministry of Community Development district officer, the district coordinator of the Ghana National Commission on Children, and three district health nurses.

"My accomplishments include helping to organize a project committee from the existing district health committee for the construction of a ten-seater Kumasi Ventilated Improved Pit (KVIP) latrine in Manso Nkwanta. In working with the traditional village council, communal labor was organized to construct the latrine. The construction was complemented by a health education seminar on sanitation.

"Additionally, I worked with the community development district officer to initiate health and sanitation education and awareness in the district through presentations and informal discussions and spent time at the district clinic assisting the community health nurses with record keeping, baby weighing, immunizations, and nutritional counseling. I also began teaching English at the local junior secondary school as a secondary service project, following water/sanitation health education.

"During my service, I enjoyed traveling to other regions of Ghana as well as surrounding countries. Another factor that made my Peace Corps experience interesting is that I lived with the royal family in my village. Since ceremonies such as the swearing in of a chief often took place in the traditional district capital, Manso Nkwanta, I was able to attend most of these events. In particular, I saw many religious holiday celebrations that predominantly consisted of prayer and dancing.

"The best advice I can give to a potential Peace Corps Volunteer," says Klug thoughtfully, "is to be patient and flexible during the whole process. Some individuals have very high or very specific expectations, and those are generally the people who quit prior to their close of service."

But those who, like Klug, maintain the right attitude echo the Peace Corps slogan: "The toughest job you'll ever love."

Meet Julia Harlan, Peace Corps Volunteer

Julia Harlan of Unionville, Indiana, is in the final year of her master's in public affairs program at Indiana University's School of Public and Environmental Affairs. Her specialized concentration is international development strategies. She earned her undergraduate degree in 1988 at Barnard College, Columbia University, majoring in American history. In 1991, she earned a law degree at the University of Wisconsin Law School. She is licensed to practice law in Tennessee and Wisconsin and will soon be sworn into the New York state bar.

"I served as a Peace Corps Volunteer from June 1995 to September 1997," says Harlan. "At the time I applied for the Peace Corps, I was working as an attorney for a private law firm. I was earning a nice salary and enjoyed the challenge of the job. However, I knew that working for a large firm wasn't the type of career I was seeking. I was interested in making a change.

"So, I started to consider my options and thought that it was an excellent time for me to undertake some sort of public service on a full-time basis. (Up to this time, I had volunteered for various nonprofit organizations.) Additionally, my mother has always been very active in volunteering her time, including serving first as a VISTA volunteer and then as a VISTA coordinator. I thought that I had the skills and education that would allow me to make a contribution, and I had the added benefit of not yet being married or owning any property, both of which require long-term commitments.

"Actually, I was not planning on joining the Peace Corps. I had hoped to become a VISTA volunteer. This was because of my mother's positive experience with the program and my belief that you don't have to leave the country to discover service opportunities. However, due to financial considerations, I decided to join the Peace Corps.

"My work as an attorney helped out enormously during my Peace Corps tenure. I had worked closely with my firm's business clients and was aware of some of the issues that face any entrepreneurs. Additionally, it helped me face situations with a diplomacy that was necessary when working in another culture. Finally, I was not overwhelmed by the amount of work I encountered, as I had come from a profession that requires major time commitments.

"Other experiences that helped me were my various kinds of volunteer service since high school. I came from a background that placed a great importance on public service. Although my father focused his energy on his job, his income afforded my mother the opportunity to serve on different boards and become very active in local activities. And at a young age my brothers and I found ourselves working as volunteers for various organizations at a variety of events. I think I just have always assumed that since I had the good fortune to be provided with a number of advantages in life, I owe something back to society in general.

"My life as a Peace Corps Volunteer varied greatly from day to day. I had two primary work sites—the regional government's Economic Development Office and the European Community's Entrepeneur Development Center. Plus, I did a number of other projects, including teaching business law at a business school and doing various development and training projects.

"Generally, I would try to help people or organizations to define issues or problems, develop a solution, and then implement this solution. Often I tried to find resources (people, training options, materials) that would benefit the client. I also became very involved in aspects of Peace Corps as an organization, serving on boards, and training new volunteers.

"My time in the Peace Corps was not dangerous, and my living standard was fine. The atmosphere in the two offices I worked in was informal and relaxed. I enjoyed working with my coworkers and hoped that they found the experience similarly rewarding. Generally, I worked a traditional forty-hour work week in the offices. I also spent a big portion of my time out of the office attending to my projects or traveling to the capital city where I taught.

"I liked the freedom I had in accomplishing my work as a volunteer. Under some very general constraints, I was able to undertake a wide variety of projects that interested me and that were beneficial to my community in Latvia. I honestly feel that I was able to provide some help to the people I worked with during my time as a volunteer. And the most positive result of my experience was discovering my interest in continuing in development work. This led me to return to school for more training so that I could pursue a career in development.

"I would advise others who are looking to serve their country to consider why they are joining the Peace Corps and what they look to get out of the experience. It seems to me that people who joined to 'save the world' were either oblivious to their underlying agendas or were trying to escape something. I think you can contribute as a volunteer but that it helps to have a micro instead of a macro viewpoint on what you can accomplish in just two years. One of my primary motivations to join was to help, but I also wanted to benefit from the experience. It was a good opportunity to learn new skills and experience a new perspective. I also hope that I accomplished some good."

Meet Dina Siber-Jaco, Peace Corps Volunteer

Dina Siber-Jaco served in the Peace Corps in Albania. Prior to her service, she earned a bachelor of arts degree in international affairs from George Washington University in Washington, D.C. After her service there, she earned a master of regional planning degree from Cornell University in Ithaca, New York. She also worked as a development worker for Los Niños, a nonprofit group promoting self-sufficiency in low-income communities in Tijuana, Mexico.

"I specialized in nutritional education for women and taught mathematics and Spanish grammar for adults working towards their elementary education diplomas," she explains.

"In my position as a Peace Corps volunteer in Albania, I specialized in English as a foreign language and youth development. I began my service in June 1992 when I was accepted to the Albania Peace Corps Program. This was the first Peace Corps program to open up in Albania, and I was selected to be one of the English teachers.

"In college and through my experiences, I had always been interested in being a part of Peace Corps and participating in their projects. After researching many organizations and after my experience working for a small nonprofit group, I wanted to be part of an organization that had a greater influence in the country of service.

"During my final year of college, I sent in three applications. The first to a graduate program in economics, with a specialty in development economics and development ethics. The second went to a small nonprofit organization, Los Niños, and the third to the Peace Corps. I was accepted into the graduate program. Consequently, I visited the school, met with the professors, and made a decision that I was too young to go to graduate school and that I needed field experience before I could tackle the questions in graduate school. I was also accepted to Los Niños, but I was still waiting for an answer from Peace Corps. Given the long application process and series of interviews necessary, I knew I could work at Los Niños for a year and then move on to the Peace Corps. My timing was correct, and in May 1992 I ended my service with Los Niños and left for Albania in June 1992.

"My previous employment was limited to work as an economic research assistant at the Economic Research Service (U.S. Department of Agriculture) and the Office of the Comptroller (U.S. Department of the Treasury) and miscellaneous internships at the Organization of American States (OAS), the United Nations Economic Commission on Latin America and the Caribbean (ECLAC), a New York publishing firm, a Washington, D.C., art gallery, and an arts magazine. For Los Niños I was a development worker.

"The most relevant experience was my work in Mexico, given that the conditions and the type of work was similar. I also felt that my other experiences were relevant since my Peace Corps experience was not only limited to English teaching. A component of the work was negotiating and finding sources of funding for new projects. For example, I was able to qualify for funding to purchase sports equipment for a girls' sports camp some fellow teachers of the community and I started. In addition, a computer was donated to my school so that I was able teach an after-school computer course to interested students.

"Given that the Peace Corps had no experience or history in Albania, volunteers were given extra freedoms in starting new programs and customizing their projects to the needs of the community. Although I was assigned as an English teacher at a local high school, I started after-school programs targeted at female high school students.

"While in Albania, I lived in a predominantly Muslim town that limited the activities of young girls and women. As the only foreigner in the community as well as a young woman close to their age, many of the girls came to me for advice or to obtain information. In developing a relationship with the girls, I found that once school ended, their activities were limited to working in the home or watching television. As a young woman, I was also limited in what I could do. (Of course, I could have done what I wanted, but I needed to maintain a professional image in order to earn respect in the community.) Given my limitations, for example on exercise, I would run in the soccer stadium adjacent to my school. Many of my students would see me and ask if they could join me. In talking to them, I found out that many of them enjoyed basketball and volleyball, and, as a result, I organized after-school basketball and volleyball games for girls.

"A typical day would go something like this:

- 7:30 A.M.—Wake up to my beeping alarm or a tap on the door.

- 8:30 A.M.—Daily gathering of teachers in the teachers room, announcement for the day.

- 9:00 A.M.—Classes begin.

- 9:00 A.M. to 1:00 P.M.—Depending on the day, I would have three to four classes, each a forty-five-minute period.

- 1:30 to 2:00 P.M.—Daily run at the soccer stadium (weather permitting).

- 2:00 P.M.—Lunch at home or sometimes a visit to a fellow colleague's home.

- 3:30 P.M.—Nap. Everyone in my host family would fall into a light afternoon nap after lunch. In my second year, I started a computer class for students (one hour).

- 4:00 to 8:00 P.M.—Weather permitting, I would play basketball with some of my students. In the winter, activities were limited to reading, preparing lessons for the next day, meeting visitors who came to my host family's home, or just talking.

- 8:00 P.M.—Dinner and the news.

- 9:00 P.M.—Reading, talking, etc.

"The actual work was only limited to the morning hours and early afternoon. Most people would work until 3:30 P.M. and then spend the rest of the time at home or with friends. It was difficult to arrange any work or meeting after these hours. Work was not very rigorous and never stressful. Although other volunteers in my Peace Corps group led busier workdays, I was limited because of the size of the town, the conservatism of the people, and the limited resources available in the town.

"The most interesting part of my work was the people I met and interacted with—my students, my host family, and the host of friends I made. Peace Corps work is not traditional in that it doesn't come to an end at 5 P.M. every day. Peace Corps really is an experience and series of events and relationships. I enjoyed just being in the country and learning about the culture, the history, the language, and the current situation. My job as a teacher was only one small part of my experience. I felt that I was an outlet for people; I was someone who they could learn from and talk to just as they were to me. We both exchanged parts of our cultures and who we were.

"Of course, there were difficult times. The most difficult was being able to do my job with extremely limited resources, if any, as well as feeling unprepared. As a volunteer, I was trained to teach intermediate-level students of English. When I arrived at my school, I was faced with classes of beginning-level students and some who had never even studied a day of English. Like all volunteers, I learned to deal with the situation and do the best that I could.

"If the Peace Corps is something you always wanted to do, then do it. Times can get difficult, so you really have to believe in your work and what you are doing. Although some people dwell on the time commitment, it is two years that you will never forget and one of the best experiences you will ever have."

Meet Kendra Spangler,
Peace Corps Volunteer

Kendra Spangler served in the Peace Corps in Suceava, Romania. "I began in June of 1997," she says, "a full year after I applied—while I was still at the State University at Albany, New York, where I earned a B.A. in Spanish in 1992. My specialty was teaching English as a Foreign Language (TEFL).

"Before entering the Peace Corps, I worked as an administrative assistant at the Abraham Fund, a nonprofit organization in New York City. I always had a romantic idea of what service in the Peace Corps would be like," she says, "roughing it in the African wilderness, helping people, etc. Although it isn't always like that, I knew that any experience would only broaden my own mind and give me a deeper understanding of the people with whom I was in contact. Besides, it seemed like the perfect time (after school) to join. I wanted Peace Corps to give me the foundation for a career in the international field.

"During my junior year at the university, I lived in Barcelona, Spain. I really enjoyed the everyday interactions and the challenges I faced living in another culture. I found that being able to speak the language put me into another level with the people. I was more respected and more accepted—not just looked upon as a tourist. This experience gave me an edge when I arrived in Romania. I acquired the language quickly and had the facilities to adapt within the society.

"For about sixteen hours each week, I teach English to middle and high school students. I run classes that are focused on communicative skills that are not generally applied in the normal English courses taught by Romanian teachers. In these classes, I teach the students about American culture and history. Also, I teach basic computer skills in English.

"The job itself is very rewarding and not in the least dangerous. I am very respected by the students and have a good working relationship with my Romanian colleagues.

"As Peace Corps volunteers teaching English, we are required to have a secondary project. I chose to teach English in a small village that does not have an English program. It has been a tremendous experience for me. When I go, I stay with a Romanian family that has adopted me as their third daughter. With them, I have been able to truly experience the ways of the Romanian people.

"My favorite part of all of this is my interaction with the children. They are eager, enthusiastic, invigorating, and extremely bright. They are the ones who recharge my batteries, so to speak. On the other side of the spectrum, it has been difficult to adjust to the Romanian timetable. Things are resolved in Romania at a much slower pace than in the United States.

"I would advise anyone who has an interest in serving in the Peace Corps to definitely try it. Every single experience is different from the next. There are surprises and disappointments, successes and frustrations, but, on the whole, it will be an experience one could never forget."

Meet Cristyn Elder,
Peace Corps Volunteer

Cristyn Elder earned a bachelor of arts degree in comparative literature with a concentration in Spanish from California State University, Long Beach, in 1993. She is in the process of earning a master of arts degree in TESOL (Teaching English to Speakers of Other Languages) from Monterey Institute of International Studies in Monterey, California.

"I worked as an EFL (English as a Foreign Language) instructor in Morelia, Michoacán, Mexico (1993-1995), at La Universidad Latina de America and at high school campuses. I taught English as a Foreign Language (EFL) and also served as an English language teacher trainer.

"I am currently working as a Peace Corps Master's Internationalist Volunteer in Ukraine. Master's Internationalists are those volunteers who join the Peace Corps after completing the first year of graduate school. Upon completing my Peace Corps tour, I will then return to graduate school to report on my work abroad as a volunteer and finish my last semester. I began my tour in Ukraine as a volunteer in June of 1997 to return to the United States in July of 1999.

"In the summer of 1992, when I was a student at California State University, Long Beach, I went on a five-week study-abroad program to Morelia, Mexico. I truly enjoyed the time I spent in Mexico and knew I wanted to go back, so after graduating from college in Spring 1993, I moved to Morelia. Upon arriving, I opened up the newspaper to look for an apartment and went down the list of schools in the phone book and started calling each one. It wasn't long before I had three teaching jobs and was turning down more. I taught EFL classes at both a private university and high school as well as a private tutoring institute. I began teaching mainly because I knew it was something I could do to support myself while living in Mexico. It started out as a way to survive, but I quickly came to realize that not only was I good at it, I also really enjoyed my students and teaching. I even started developing my own teaching materials and conducted training workshops for my colleagues.

"Due to the decrease in the value of the peso and because I knew I wanted to go to graduate school, I decided to return to California in 1995. I decided to study TESOL because I was good at teaching and felt that being an EFL teacher was my ticket around the world. I could go just about anywhere and support myself through teaching. When I applied to the Monterey Institute of International Studies, I found out that they offered a degree in TESOL that could also be combined with serving as a Peace Corps Volunteer. (I receive four units toward my degree for being in the Peace Corps as well as a scholarship for my last eleven units.)

"My initial reason for joining the Peace Corps was that I wanted to share the education I received at Monterey with those who do not have access to the same educational opportunities. In addition, I saw learning a new language, learning about a new culture, and traveling as great benefits to the job.

"I am currently working as a Peace Corps TEFL (Teaching English as a Foreign Language) Volunteer in Kherson, Ukraine. My primary site is the Southern Ukraine Regional In-service Teacher Training Institute, where I conduct teacher-development courses for Ukrainian English teachers. The courses run for three weeks, four times a year. During the 'down time' between courses, I teach EFL at a secondary school six hours per week. I have a class of sixth graders and ninth graders on Monday, Tuesday, and Wednesday. I fill up the rest of my week with various tasks, such as developing materials and conducting workshops and seminars in other cities around Ukraine. I have just completed writing a teacher-training manual that describes my work involving the courses. The manual is written to be used by less-experienced and less-educated TEFL volunteers who will be working in a teacher training capacity. I have also just completed a pilot project with Oxford University Press for the new textbook, *Open Doors*. Also, a fellow volunteer and I are now working on an AIDS-education curriculum for secondary schools in Ukraine.

"I am a very fortunate volunteer in that my Ukrainian counterparts at both the training institute and the secondary school are very supportive and encourage me in all my projects.

"One reason I love teaching is because I am not required to work from nine to five (and, of course, I have great summer and winter vacations). The hours I spend at the secondary school and the teacher training courses are really the only set schedule I have. The rest of the day (or month), I dictate how and on what projects my time will be spent. Also, I love working with students and other teachers. The students keep me young and let me know what is happening with the 'new generation.' Also, because I am a teacher trainer, I am required to stay up-to-date with the latest theories and trends in teaching. Furthermore, my job is never the same on a day-to-day basis, and it provides me with a creative outlet.

"What I like least about my job is that I can never stop thinking about what I have to plan for tomorrow. Also, unlike some jobs, I have to take my work home with me every night—whether it's to correct students' papers or to plan for the next day. I'm also disappointed that teaching is not seen as a more prestigious profession. I think many people in society don't realize what an influence teachers have on their children, the next generation. Teachers not only teach their subjects but also teach cultural values and help students develop their social skills. Sadly enough, teachers often spend more time raising other people's children for them. What is even worse is that it is often said that the best teachers are usually the first ones to quit teaching.

"Following in my footsteps may mean one of two things— becoming an EFL teacher and/or a Peace Corps volunteer. In either case, I would suggest that you ask a teacher in a local school or college, etc., if you could observe some classes and even take time to interview different teachers about the profession. Finally, I would recommend volunteering as a teacher's aide or as an English language teacher at a local church or a nonprofit literacy organization to test out whether you might enjoy teaching. However, be forewarned. Just because you may find you don't enjoy teaching primary students or adults, for example, it doesn't mean you wouldn't enjoy teaching high school kids or international university students.

"I really enjoy my job as an EFL instructor, teacher trainer, and Peace Corps Volunteer. I'm one of the lucky people who likes going to work every day. It is more of a hobby than a chore. My ideal job after I finish my tour in Ukraine and upon graduating from the Monterey Institute of International Studies is to work during the regular academic year as an EFL instructor with international university students or Mexican children who have immigrated to the United States. Then, in order to stay current in my profession and to keep my travel bug satiated, I'd like to conduct teacher-training workshops abroad during the summer."

For Additional Information

Check your phone book for regional recruiting offices or contact:

Peace Corps
1990 K Street NW, Room 9320
Washington, DC 20526
1-800-424-8580

CHAPTER SIX

Careers in Politics and Government

"Politics is the art of the possible." OTTO VON BISMARCK

D
oes a government or political job hold some interest for you? If so, you will be pleased to hear that these kinds of positions are available for you to pursue at the local, state, and federal levels.

Government jobs are available in the following areas: agriculture, animal control, aquariums and zoos, code administration and enforcement, computers, engineering and science, environment, fire protection, fleet and facilities management, forestry and horticulture, law enforcement, legal services and the courts, library services, media and the arts, parks and recreation, planning, community and economic development, housing, landscape architecture, public administration, public health and health care, public safety, public works, records management, social services, transportation and traffic, and utilities management.

Political Jobs

At the top of the political hierarchy are public office holders, including mayors, governors, supervisors, senators, representatives, and, of course, the president and vice president of the country. All of these individuals are elected to administer government. They handle all of the business of a city, town, state, county, or the country as a whole. They must pass laws to keep order, set up special programs to benefit people, and spend the taxpayers' money on goods and services. As problem solvers, they meet with community leaders to find out the needs of the people, and then they search for ways to meet those needs.

There are many other levels of political careers—all the way down to the local levels. This would include those who work for political change in their neighborhoods and those in an official capacity, such as precinct captain. Some of these jobs are voluntary, unpaid positions that could eventually lead to paying positions.

All positions except appointed government managers are elected by their constituents. Nonelected managers are hired by a local government council or commission.

Chief Executives and Legislators

Government chief executives, like their counterparts in the private sector, have overall responsibility for the performance of their organizations. Working in conjunction with legislators, they set goals and then organize programs to attain them. They appoint department heads who oversee the work of the civil servants who carry out programs and enforce laws enacted by their legislative bodies. They oversee budgets specifying how government resources will be used and ensure that resources are used properly and programs are carried out as planned.

Routinely, chief executives meet with legislators and constituents to discuss proposed programs and determine their levels of support. They frequently confer with leaders of other governments to solve mutual problems. Sometimes they have to make painful and difficult decisions, such as breaking diplomatic relationships with other countries or even declare war.

Chief executives nominate citizens to boards and commissions, solicit bids from and select contractors to do work for the government, encourage business investment and economic development in their jurisdictions, and seek federal or state funds.

Chief executives of large jurisdictions rely on a staff of aides and assistants, but those in small jurisdictions often must do much of the work themselves.

Legislators are the elected officials who pass or amend laws. They include United States senators and representatives, state senators and representatives, county legislators, and city and town council members.

Legislators may introduce bills in the legislative body and examine and vote on bills introduced by other legislators. They often make decisions on issues such as the types of weapons the country will need for defense, how much money should be spent on the space program, and how to protect the environment. In preparing legislation, they read staff reports and may work with constituents, representatives of interest groups, members of boards and commissions, the chief executive and department heads, and others with an interest in the legislation. They generally must approve budgets and the appointments of department heads and commission members submitted by the chief executive. In some jurisdictions, the legislative body appoints a city, town, or county manager. Many legislators, especially at the state and federal levels, have a staff to perform research, prepare legislation, and help resolve constituents' problems.

Both chief executives and legislators perform many ceremonial duties such as opening new buildings, making proclamations, welcoming visitors, and leading celebrations. It is both a privilege and an important responsibility to serve in public office.

Government Jobs

Government positions are available for those in a variety of occupations—everything from administrative assistants to law enforcers to computer programmers. Jobs are available at local, state, and federal levels. The federal government, which has a very systematized system of hiring, offers positions in the following five general categories:

* Professional occupations

* Administrative occupations

* Technical occupations

* Clerical occupations

* Other occupations

A Sample Federal Job Announcement

Open Competition Announcement: Accountant.
Duty location: Parkersburg, West Virginia. For application information, contact:

Bureau of the Public Debt
200 Third Street, Room 206-1
Parkersburg, WV 26106-1328

Promotion potential to GS-12. Announcement contains qualification requirements and ranking factors. Application must be postmarked by closing date. Some substitution of education or experience is permissible.

Organization: Office of Public Debt Accounting, Division of Accounting Operations, Government Securities Management Branch.

Duty Station: Parkersburg, West Virginia. Salary Range: GS-5 to GS-7 (about $20,500 to $25,500).

Additional requirements: For the GS-5: None. For the GS-7: Specialized experience: fifty-two weeks of experience equivalent to the GS-5 level that is directly related to the position to be filled and that has equipped the candidate with the particular knowledge, skills, and abilities to successfully perform the duties of the position. Or education (including copy of transcript or a list of college courses including the number of credit hours earned to ensure proper credit): One full year of graduate-level education in either accounting or auditing or related fields, such as business administration, finance, or public administration; or superior academic achievement demonstrated through class standing, grade point average, or election to membership in a national scholastic honor society. Some substitution of education for experience is permissible.

Eligibility requirements: Applicant must be a United States citizen.

Basis of ranking: Qualified applicants will be rated on how their experience relates to the following:

1. Ability to learn the application of professional accounting standards, practices, policies, and procedures.

2. Knowledge of computerized and manual accounting systems.

3. Ability to interact effectively with others within and outside the organization.

4. Ability to communicate effectively in writing.

5. Ability to communicate effectively to present facts, ideas, and concepts.

How to apply: In order to be considered, you must submit an application (Optional Application for Federal Employment, OF-612; Application for Federal Employment, SF-171; resume).

You must enclose a copy of your college transcript or a list of college courses including the number of credit hours earned.

Complete packages must be submitted (or postmarked) by date noted. Applications will not be returned. Candidates will not be solicited for further experience/education background data or for proof of veteran experience if the information provided is found to be incomplete or inadequate. Candidates will be notified of the results following selection by the hiring agency.

Equal employment opportunity: All candidates will be considered without discrimination for any non-merit reason such as race.

More Government Job Opportunities

Jobs for the federal government also include working for the various departments of government, such as the Department of Agriculture, Department of Defense, Department of Justice, Department of the Interior, Department of State, the United States Treasury Department, the Department of Veterans Affairs, and many others.

Each major department includes a number of subdepartments. The Department of the Interior, for instance, includes the Fish and Wildlife Service, the Bureau of Indian Affairs, the Bureau of Land Management, and the National Park Service. Opportunities for government or political jobs may be found throughout the country in federal, state, and local offices.

Working Conditions

The working conditions of chief executives and legislators vary with the size and budget of the governmental unit. Time spent at work ranges from meeting once a month for a local council member to sixty or more hours per week for a United States senator.

United States senators and representatives, governors and lieutenant governors, and chief executives and legislators in large local jurisdictions usually work full-time year-round, as do county and city managers. Many state legislators work full-time while legislatures are in session (usually for two to six months a year) and part-time the rest of the year. Local elected officials in many jurisdictions work a schedule that is officially designated part-time but actually is the equivalent of a full-time schedule when unpaid duties are taken into account.

In addition to their regular schedules, chief executives are on call at all hours to handle emergencies.

Some jobs require occasional out-of-town travel, but others involve long periods away from home to attend sessions of the legislature.

Qualifications and Training

Voters seek to elect the individual believed to be most qualified from among a number of candidates who meet the minimum age, residency, and citizenship requirements. There are no formal educational requirements for public office holders. However, successful candidates must be able to show the people that they are qualified for the jobs they seek, and a good education is one of the best qualifications a candidate can offer.

Successful candidates usually have a strong record of accomplishment in paid and unpaid work in their districts. Some have business, teaching, or legal experience, but others come from a wide variety of occupations. In addition, many have experience as members of boards or commissions. Some candidates become well known for work with charities, political action groups, political campaigns, or with religious, fraternal, and social organizations.

Management-level work experience and public service help develop the planning, organizing, negotiating, motivating, fundraising, budgeting, public speaking, and problem-solving skills needed to run an effective political campaign. Candidates must make decisions quickly, sometimes on the basis of limited or contradictory information. They must inspire and motivate their constituents and their staffs. They need to appear sincere and candid and able to present their views thoughtfully and convincingly. Additionally, they must know how to hammer out compromises and satisfy the demands of constituents. National and statewide campaigns require massive amounts of energy and stamina, as well as superior fund-raising skills.

Town, city, and county managers are generally hired by a council or commission. Managers come from a variety of educational backgrounds. A master's degree in public administration, including courses such as public financial management and legal issues in public administration, is widely recommended. Virtually all town, city, and county managers have at least a bachelor's degree, and the majority hold a master's degree. Working in management support positions in government is a prime source of the experience and personal contacts required in eventually securing a manager position.

Generally, a town, city, or county manager in a smaller jurisdiction is required to have expertise in a wide variety of areas. Those who work for larger jurisdictions specialize in financial, administrative, and personnel matters. For all managers, communication skills and the ability to get along with others are essential.

Advancement opportunities for elected public officials are not clearly defined. Because elected positions normally require a period of residency and local public support is critical, officials can usually advance to other offices only in the jurisdictions where they live. For example, council members may run for mayor or for a position in the state government, and state legislators may run for governor or for Congress. Many officials are not overly politically ambitious, however, and do not seek advancement. Others lose their bids for reelection or voluntarily leave the occupation. A lifetime career as a government chief executive or legislator is rare except for those who reach the national level.

Town, city, and county managers have a better defined career path. They generally obtain a master's degree in public administration, then gain experience as management analysts or assistants in government departments working for committees, councils, or chief executives. They learn about planning, budgeting, civil engineering, and other aspects of running a government. With sufficient experience, they may be hired to manage a small government and often move on to manage progressively larger governments over time.

Educational/training requirements for government positions will vary considerably, depending on the nature of the job and the duties involved. Qualifications for jobs with the federal government will be spelled out in the appropriate job notice.

Salaries for Political Jobs

Earnings of public administrators vary widely, depending on the size of the government unit and on whether the job is part-time, full-time and year-round, or full-time for only a few months a year. Salaries range from little or nothing for a small town council member to $200,000 a year for the president of the United States. According to the International City/County Management Association, the average annual salary of chief elected county officials in 1996 was $25,600, while chief elected city officials earned about $12,200. ICMA data indicate that the average salary for city managers was about $70,600 in 1996, while that of county managers was about $86,700.

According to the National Conference of State Legislatures, the salary for legislators in the forty states that paid an annual salary ranged from about $10,000 to $47,000 per year. In six states, legislators received a daily salary plus an allowance for expenses while legislatures were in session. Two states paid no expenses and only nominal daily salaries, while two states paid no salary at all but did pay a daily expense allowance. Salaries and the expense allowance were generally higher in the larger states.

Data from *Book of the States, 1996–97*, indicate that gubernatorial annual salaries ranged from $60,000 in Arkansas to $130,000 in New York. In addition to a salary, most governors received perquisites such as transportation and an official residence. In 1997, U.S. senators and representatives earned $133,600, the Senate and House majority and minority leaders $148,400, and the vice president $171,500.

Salaries for Government Jobs

Salaries for government jobs are based upon General Schedule (GS) ratings. Here are some typical figures, though many cities, where cost-of-living is higher than average, offer higher salaries. As of January 1999, federal pay levels followed this schedule:

GS-1 $13,362 per year

GS-2 $15,023 per year

GS-3 $16,392 per year

GS-4 $18,401 per year

GS-5 $20,588 per year

GS-6 $22,948 per year

GS-7 $25,501 per year

GS-8 $28,242 per year

GS-9 $31,195 per year

GS-10 $34,353 per year

GS-11 $37,744 per year

GS-12 $45,236 per year

GS-13	$53,793 per year
GS-14	$63,567 per year
GS-15	$74,773 per year

Meet Karen Sweeny-Justice, National Park Ranger

Karen Sweeny-Justice earned an A.A.S. Degree in graphic art from Onondaga Community College in Syracuse, New York, an A.A. in communications from Cazenovia College in Cazenovia, New York, and a B.S. in human development from Syracuse University in New York.

She serves as a national park ranger-interpretation (Big South Fork National River and Recreation Area, Tennessee and Kentucky) and has been associated with the park service for more than twelve years. During that time, she completed a number of courses with the National Park Service and National Career Workshops, including the following: Developing African-American Interpretive Programs, Interpretation for Children, Self-Study Course for Interpreters, Interpretation in Urban Areas, Ranger Skills, How to Supervise People, Management Skills for Success in the 1990s, How to Work with People, Orientation to the Management of National Park System Resources, along with first aid and safety courses.

"After working in a bank as a financial sales counselor for more than two years, I decided I needed a change," she says, "so I quit that job and, sight unseen, accepted a position for a lot less money as a summer employee at the Old Faithful Lodge in Yellowstone National Park. I used the chance to be in the park as a basis for exploration of the region, and, discovering that I was one of the 'older' concession employees (at the ripe old age of twenty-eight), I decided I needed something that would get me out of the dorm. So when I learned that the park service needed volunteers, I signed on to work at the Old Faithful Visitor Center. The rangers I worked with were informative and trusted me enough to let me solo on explanations of what was going on. I even got good at predicting when Old Faithful would erupt.

"While I still worked at the lodge, the visitor center experience was what led to my future. At Yellowstone, I learned about a group called the Student Conservation Association, and I signed on to volunteer with them that winter. I was selected by Biscayne National Park and spent the winter down in Florida doing the same work that the seasonal rangers did. That included presenting programs like glass-bottom boat tours and staffing the visitor centers.

"Basically, I discovered I liked the chance to help visitors better understand the parks they were in. Besides, I've always liked talking to people! Many of the other rangers I know started out as volunteers, so the path I took isn't that unique.

"There was nothing in my past experience that would have indicated that I'd like parks. I grew up in a city and am the only one of my family that has left. And not only have I left my home town, I've traveled and worked in a variety of locations in the past twelve years, including Yellowstone, Biscayne, Shenandoah, Lowell, Valley Forge, and Big South Fork.

"Some parks are busier than others," she explains. "While an urban park like Valley Forget might see more than one thousand visitors on a Saturday, a park in a rural area (that one must really drive to get to), might have fewer than a hundred visitors. Park seasons vary, too. Yellowstone is mostly summer, while the Everglades is mostly winter. It all depends on the weather and natural conditions. So, some days it may be boring and slow, allowing lots of time to do research, while on other days one may not even get a chance for lunch.

"Interpretation isn't dangerous, but, on occasion, one may be asked to help with medical emergencies and search and rescues,"

Sweeny-Justice continues. "Some parks have different shifts that need to be covered, and sometimes that means opening or closing buildings alone.

"Forty-hour work weeks are the norm, although if staff is slim, there may be overtime. The atmosphere varies from park to park. And each park does get its share of visitors who think that because rangers are public servants, they can be walked over, ignored, or abused. It doesn't happen often, but it does happen. I've had people shout and yell at me and call me names. On the other hand, I've received lots of praise from people who have enjoyed the programs I've done well enough to send letters to my supervisors.

"The upsides of the job are the feelings that come when you can see someone grasping a concept they didn't understand before or helping someone to make the most of a visit. Getting to see the treasures our nation offers is a benefit, too. It used to be said that rangers were 'paid in sunsets.'

"The downsides are the fact that the pay isn't spectacular, people don't always use their common sense when they're on vacation, and there is a lot of work in buildings that can be very uncomfortable. For example, I worked year-round in a historic Washington's Headquarters at Valley Forge. The building was built in the eighteenth century, didn't have a modern heating/cooling system, and had only one bare lightbulb hanging in the stairwell behind the door to the basement. Needless to say, it wasn't very comfortable.

"Working for the park service can be mentally draining, especially if you want to make it a career. I say this because it is very competitive, and there are no guarantees that permanent employment will come to you. I had to take a job as a permanent secretary to get my 'status' to apply for permanent ranger positions. And as a seasonal employee, you don't get any benefits like insurance and can be let go at any time. Right now, I have a friend who has been working as a temporary employee for more

114 CAREERS FOR PATRIOTIC TYPES

than ten years, and she only knows that she has a job until March 1999. Another friend who has been in a similar situation was very lucky just to compete successfully for her job, and she is now permanent.

"If you don't like speaking to total strangers or giving programs to audiences that range from a few people to crowds of more than a hundred, you wouldn't really enjoy this job. But for those of us who do—it's perfect!"

Meet Vera Marie Badertscher, Campaign Manager and Campaign Consultant

Vera Marie Badertscher earned a bachelor of arts degree and a bachelor of science degree in education from Ohio State University in 1960. Her major was theater/English. She went on to secure a master of fine arts degree from Arizona State University in 1976, focusing on theater.

"Originally I served as campaign manager for many years," Badertscher says. "More recently I have been employed as a campaign consultant.

"I started as a citizen volunteer in city projects," she explains. "As a young mother, I wanted a better library system in Scottsdale, Arizona, where I lived, so I volunteered for a committee. There I met office holders, was invited to serve on their advisory committees, and eventually asked and received pay for managing a city council election campaign.

"I enjoyed the sense of accomplishment of working in politics—of being able to promote my beliefs and make things happen," she says. "I also enjoyed the fact that most people involved in politics are action oriented, optimistic true believers. My chief asset was an ability to figure out the best way to communicate political messages and move people to action.

"My volunteer work in a federated woman's club gave me experience in bringing diverse people together to work on projects;

combining government and private energies; communicating; and organizing projects. My theater background helped me focus on short-term, collaborative projects.

"As a campaign manager, I spent most of my time communicating with volunteers—mostly on the phone but sometimes in memos or in newsletters. It is a very intense job because of the limited time for a political campaign (usually about nine months—perhaps symbolic). Someone advised me when I managed my first congressional campaign that during the last couple of weeks of the campaign, I would be making a dozen decisions every hour and one in twenty or so would be truly important.

"Prioritizing is critical in political campaigns," she stresses. "You need to know the difference between decisions that do not affect the outcome (what color the signs are) and decisions that do (should the candidate attend a particular debate)?

"A campaign manager rounds up diverse interest groups, volunteers, the candidate and his or her family, advertising personnel, researchers, and fund-raisers. The key to being successful is keeping the focus on what will get the candidate elected and not allowing anyone in the campaign to draw the focus in another direction. You can expect to talk on the phone all day, check off on other people's work, and stay close to the candidate to keep him or her on track. Generally, you are trying to keep the budget down, so the work surroundings are on the primitive side— borrowed furniture and unpainted walls. You can count on noise and constant activity. (If it's quiet, you're probably losing.) This presents a hard atmosphere to concentrate in, but that's the job.

"A campaign consultant has more luxury of time to think than does a campaign manager. The consultant typically analyzes voting data history; studies the candidate, the opponent, and the voters; and writes a strategic plan for bringing the voters to support that candidate. Some consultants specialize in media or mail, but I have been a generalist, doing strategy and writing direct mail. The consultant works in an office or home office and meets weekly or biweekly with the candidate, the campaign manager, and others involved in the campaign. Once the plan is written, the consultant is available to help with fine-tuning, to help make adjustments, to help review media plans, to help determine what to ask in polling, and to help interpret the results. While the campaign manager's job is not done until the polls close on election day, the consultant's job is done a few days prior to the election when no more mail can be sent or advertising launched that will affect the outcome.

"I most like the ability to work out the puzzles involved in bringing together the circumstances, the candidate, and the voters in order to persuade them that they will be better off to elect that candidate. I like the thinking and the communicating of politics.

"What I least like is having to be nice to a bunch of people that I might not particularly like or admire. However, I have been fortunate in being able to choose the candidates I work for, so I have worked for people I believe in and personally support. However, politics is about coalition building, so sometimes the expression 'politics makes strange bedfellows' is all too true.

"I am frustrated with the general disdain for politics and the growing cynicism, which I fear will damage our democracy," she says. "So, I would like to be able to persuade people that there are good and worthy people in elected office. My hat is truly off to the people who do participate—by voting or by running for office or by supporting those who run.

"I would advise anyone interested in entering this kind of work to introduce yourself to a candidate you admire and volunteer to help. Political science classes teach theory, but only campaigning teaches campaigning. Don't try to tell the candidate how to run his or her campaign or volunteer to be the brains behind the organization until you have actually done some of the grunt work of campaigning and learned it from the inside out. You'd be surprised how many people come to a campaign manager and say,

'I'm really good at strategy,' when all the campaign manager really needs is someone to go out in a pickup truck and put up signs. And before any of that—register to vote. Read up on the issues. And last but not least—VOTE!"

Meet Wade Hyde, Political Consultant

Wade Hyde earned a bachelor of arts degree in education and history from East Texas State University in Commerce. He continued his education and received a master of arts degree in urban affairs from the University of Texas at Arlington. He also earned a master of arts degree in civic affairs teaching from the University of Dallas in Irving, Texas. He has served as a campaign manager volunteer consultant, as a civic volunteer board member, and as a planning and zoning commission member in Irving for four years. Currently, he serves as a member of the regional transportation board and member and officer of the Visiting Nurses Association.

"In 1980, I began volunteering in organizations supporting interests with legislative agendas," he says. "Political events were at the center of what I found to be most interesting and exciting in earlier years. These events included listening to the presidential nominating conventions (before pollsters and analysts took all the fun and suspense out of final outcomes) on the radio and waiting in the town square for the results of local elections on hot June Saturday nights.

"History studies and government were naturally interesting and easy for me. No other subject particularly intrigued me. Politics and policy are my calling.

"Attending the unique program at the university, now called the Institute of Culture and Humanities, cofounded by Dr. James Hillman, was an eye- and mind-opening experience. The course of study encouraged use of the imagination and image of the heart.

"Political consulting is seasonal work, and the season can last for three months to two years depending on the type of campaign—local, regional or national," Hyde explains. "Political campaigning at a local level is extremely concentrated, normally three months, entered into by a candidate who has sometimes given very little serious thought about preparation of voter lists, coalition building, fund-raising, or issue presentation. The nature of the political candidate is usually one of tremendous energy and strong ego with an unshakable belief that the voting populace cannot live without his or her leadership. The consultant, on the other hand, must bring some order and a consistent, coherent message to the candidate and the workers. The atmosphere is one of chaotic, pressure-cooker days and nights.

"Everything is always late, unexpected, and includes last-minute and last-second decision making—sometimes like flipping a coin and forging ahead or backtracking. The days start as if the nights had never quit, and each workday lasts about eighteen hours. Both the candidate and campaign workers contract battle fatigue that doesn't end until weeks after election day. Saturdays and Sundays are not exempt.

"Each new campaign and candidate comes with the promise of a better day and a better way. It's exciting and hopeful to be involved in making a positive change by helping elect someone who can make a big difference. At least that's the upside. The downside is the exhaustion and condensed pressure of a compact campaign effort and, if such should occur, the loss of the candidate's best effort.

"I would advise others interested in entering this field to understand fully and honestly why you are working for a candidate. Know if you're primarily in it for a job, an appointment, for the experience and excitement, or for the candidate. Be realistic and don't hang around too long because burnout can set in quite soon. See *Wag the Dog* and *Primary Colors*—I found them to be pretty accurate as campaign compilations."

Meet K. Mark Takai, State Representative

K. Mark Takai earned a bachelor of arts degree in political science in 1990 and a master of public health degree in health education in 1993 from the University of Hawaii at Manoa, Honolulu. During his internship for his master's degree, he worked for a city council member for the city and county of Honolulu.

"My experiences at the University of Hawaii while an undergraduate student, graduate student, and employee probably attracted me to the state capitol," he says. "It was through these years that I had the most interaction with the legislators. I now serve as an elected state representative representing District 34, part of Aiea and part of Pearl City (both located near Pearl Harbor on Oahu).

"The job of an elected official interested me from when I was a young child (probably from fourth grade, when I was involved in student government). I continued to be involved with student government in high school, serving as the student body president for a 2,400-student school and in college as the student body representing more than 12,000 students. I truly enjoy all opportunities to interact with people from diverse backgrounds and interests.

"I declared my candidacy for public office in July 1994, won the primary election in September, and was declared the winner of the seat after the general election in November.

"The job of a state representative runs the gamut. There are probably three different 'jobs' of an elected official—very diverse, but all very important. The first is my job as a community leader. This is probably the most rewarding part of being in public office. The interaction with the community—through the schools, community organizations, neighborhood board meetings, and so forth—all provide me with the opportunity to listen and then respond to the desires and concerns of the public.

"This part of the job can also be very difficult. In the more than four years since first being elected, I have been very fortunate in that I have not had too many difficult meetings with the public; however, as a freeway project is currently being planned and the project calls for possible public condemnation of private property, I have had my fair share of angry constituents. Most times, though, I am able to work with the residents of our community to address their concerns.

"The second part of my job is as a lawmaker. Constitutionally, this is my most important responsibility. Seventy-five legislators decide what laws are passed.

"My third responsibility is as a politician (i.e., a political candidate). State house offices are up every two years, so since my first election in 1994, I have had to run two reelection campaigns. This is a very time-consuming process. The 'campaign season' begins around July of even-numbered years and doesn't end until the general election in early November. Aside from raising money to run a successful campaign (marketing materials, brochures, advertisements, etc.), the most difficult and time-consuming tasks of the political season are sign waving (waving to cars along the roadside in the mornings and afternoons) and door-to-door canvassing.

"A typical day for me depends on the time of year. During the legislative session (January to May), a typical day begins at 7:30 A.M. with a breakfast. Then it's off to the state capitol for committee meetings that begin at 8:30 or 9 A.M. We have private meetings in our offices or we catch up on phone calls before the House floor session at noon. Then it's time to eat lunch with constituents or go to a luncheon after the session. At 2 P.M. we start our committee hearings, which usually run until 7 P.M. After the committee hearings, I usually participate in community meetings, which usually run to 10 P.M.

"I usually keep Friday evenings free from office work and routinely spend that time with my wife. Saturdays are generally busy with committee hearings or community events. Sundays are typically days reserved for family activities.

"During the off-election year, nonsession months, I usually work in the office planning for upcoming events. As the state cochairman of Hawaii's Children and Youth in October for the past three years and as the state cochairman of Hawaii's Junior Miss Scholarship Program in January for the past two years, I find myself sometimes even busier than during the legislative session.

"The period of nonsession months during the campaign season is really tough and grueling. And, including time spent at receptions, dinners, and so on, I probably spend about seventy hours a week working. However, the people I work with (both in the state capitol and throughout the community) make my job most rewarding. I would not trade the experiences that I have had for any other job. Although it can be very stressful and time consuming, I truly enjoy my job as a state representative.

"I derive great pleasure from doing for others. For instance, one of my most rewarding moments occurred when I was able to provide assistance in getting funds to build a new traffic signal at an intersection that saw many near accidents, numerous accidents, and one fatality.

"The least enjoyable part of my job is knowing full well that every bill that we pass and that becomes law has a negative impact on someone or on a specific profession. Although I have voted for many bills that do much good for our community overall, sometimes it is these same bills that get people laid off from their jobs, and so forth. Knowing this causes me great pain.

"I would encourage anyone interested in pursuing this kind of career to talk to people about what their concerns are. Meet with various community leaders in your community. Get involved with political campaigns and/or volunteer or work for an elected official. And if you are truly serious, begin your plans for an eventual run for public office. Good luck!"

For Additional Information

Information on appointed officials in local government can be obtained from:

International City/County Management Association
777 North Capitol Street NE, Suite 500
Washington, DC 20002

Here are some additional resources:

Democratic National Committee
Young Democrats of America
430 South Capitol Street SE
Washington, DC 20003

Republication National Committee
310 First Street SE
Washington, DC 20003

The Congressional Management Foundation
513 Capitol Court NE, Suite 100
Washington, DC 20002

Websites

United States Office of Personnel Management
http://www.opm.gov/index.htm

This is the home page you'll want to study if you are interested in federal positions. It contains a plethora of general information, listings of current jobs openings, on-line applications, and other useful forms.

http://www.jobweb.org

Click on the "jobs" button and you'll find government jobs listed. It's also worthwhile to look through the listing of "Directory of Employers."

http://www.jobweb.org/catapult/catapult.htm

This site provides links to resources for federal as well as state and local government jobs.

Office of Personnel Management's Federal Employment Information Centers

Located throughout the country, these are the best places to obtain information and location openings.

ALABAMA
Federal Employment Information Center
3322 Memorial Parkway South
Huntsville, AL 35801

ALASKA
Federal Employment Information Center
222 West Seventh Avenue
Anchorage, AK 99513

ARIZONA
Federal Employment Information Center
Century Plaza Building, Room 1415
3225 North Central Avenue
Phoenix, AZ 85012

ARKANSAS
(Contact the San Antonio, Texas, center)

CALIFORNIA
Federal Employment Information Center
Los Angeles Area
9650 Flair Drive
El Monte, CA 91731

Federal Employment Information Center
Federal Building
1029 J Street
Sacramento, CA 95814
(Kiosk Location)

Federal Employment Information Center
211 Main Street
Second Floor, Room 235
San Francisco, CA 94120

COLORADO
Federal Employment Information Center
P.O. Box 25167
Denver, CO 80225

CONNECTICUT
Federal Building
450 Main Street
Hartford, CT
(Kiosk Location; or contact Massachusetts center)

DELAWARE
(Contact the Philadelphia, Pennsylvania, center)

DISTRICT OF COLUMBIA
Federal Employment Information Center
1900 E Street NW
Washington, DC 20415
(Kiosk Location)

FLORIDA
Federal Employment Information Center
3444 McCrory Place
Orlando, FL 32803

GEORGIA
Federal Employment Information Center
Richard B. Russell Federal Building
75 Spring Street SW, Suite 956
Atlanta, GA 30303

GUAM
Federal Employment Information Center
Pacific Daily News Building
Agana, Guam 96910

HAWAII
Federal Employment Information Center
Federal Building
300 Ala Moana Boulevard
Honolulu, HI 96850
(Kiosk Location)

IDAHO
(Contact the Seattle, Washington, center)

ILLINOIS
Information Center
175 West Jackson
Chicago, IL 60604
(Kiosk Location)

INDIANA
Federal Employment Information Center
Minton Capehart Federal Building
575 North Pennsylvania Street
Indianapolis, IN 46204
(Kiosk Location)

IOWA
(Contact the Kansas City, Missouri, center)

KANSAS
Federal Employment Information Center
One-Twenty Building
120 South Market Street
Wichita, KS 67202

KENTUCKY
(Contact the Dayton, Ohio, center)

LOUISIANA
Federal Employment Information Center
1515 Poydras Street
New Orleans, LA 70112

MAINE
Federal Building
40 Western Avenue
Augusta, ME 04330
(Kiosk Location; or contact the Boston, Massachusetts, center)

MARYLAND
Federal Employment Information Center
300 West Pratt Street
Baltimore, MD 21201

MASSACHUSETTS
Federal Employment Information Center
Federal Building
10 Causeway Street
Boston, MA 02222
(Kiosk Location)

MICHIGAN
Federal Employment Information Center
477 Michigan Avenue
Detroit, MI 48226

MINNESOTA
Federal Employment Information Center
Federal Building
1 Federal Drive
Twin Cities, MN 55111
(Kiosk Location)

MISSISSIPPI
(Contact the Huntsville, Alabama, center)

MISSOURI
Federal Employment Information Center
Federal Building
601 East Twelfth Street
Kansas City, MO 64106
(Kiosk Location)

MONTANA
(Contact the Denver, Colorado, center)

NEBRASKA
(Contact the Wichita, Kansas, center)

NEVADA
(Contact the Sacramento or Los Angeles, California, centers)

NEW HAMPSHIRE
(Contact the Boston, Massachusetts, center)

NEW JERSEY
Federal Building
970 Broad Street
Newark, NJ 07102
(Kiosk Location; or contact New York City or Philadelphia,
    Pennsylvania, centers)

NEW MEXICO
Federal Employment Information Center
Federal Building
505 Marquette Avenue
Albuquerque, NM 87102

NEW YORK
Federal Employment Information Center
Jacob B. Javits Federal Building
26 Federal Plaza
New York, NY 10278
(Kiosk Location)

Federal Employment Information Center
James M. Hanley Federal Building
100 South Clinton Street
Syracuse, NY 13260
(Kiosk Location)

NORTH CAROLINA
Federal Employment Information Center
4407 Bland Road
Raleigh, NC 27609
(Kiosk Location)

NORTH DAKOTA
(Contact the Twin Cities, Minnesota, center)

OHIO
Federal Employment Information Center
Federal Building
200 West Second Street
Dayton, OH 45402
(Kiosk Location)

OKLAHOMA
(Contact the San Antonio, Texas, center)

OREGON
Federal Employment Information Center
Federal Building
1220 SW Third Avenue
Portland, OR 97204

PENNSYLVANIA
Federal Employment Information Center
Federal Building
228 Walnut Street
Harrisburg, PA 17108
(Kiosk Location)

Federal Employment Information Center
Federal Building
600 Arch Street
Philadelphia, PA 19106
(Kiosk Location)

Federal Employment Information Center
Federal Building
1000 Liberty Avenue
Pittsburgh, PA 15222

PUERTO RICO
Federal Employment Information Center
Federal Building
150 Carlos Chardon Avenue
Hato Rey, San Juan, PR 00918
(Kiosk Location)

RHODE ISLAND
380 Westminster
Providence, RI 02903
(Kiosk Location; or contact the Boston, Massachusetts, center)

SOUTH CAROLINA
(Contact the Raleigh, North Carolina, center)

SOUTH DAKOTA
(Contact the Twin Cities, Minnesota, center)

TENNESSEE
Federal Employment Information Center
200 Jefferson Avenue
Memphis, TN 38103

TEXAS
Federal Employment Information Center
1100 Commerce Street
Dallas, TX 75242
(Kiosk Location)

Federal Employment Information Center
8610 Broadway
San Antonio, TX 78217

UTAH
(Contact Colorado FEIC Listing)

VERMONT
Federal Building
11 Elmwood Avenue
Burlington, VT 05401
(Kiosk Location; or contact the Boston, Massachusetts, center)

VIRGIN ISLANDS
(Contact San Juan, Puerto Rico, center)

VIRGINIA
Federal Employment Information Center
Federal Building
220 Granby Mall
Norfolk, VA 23510-1886
(Kiosk Location)

WASHINGTON
Federal Employment Information Center
Federal Building
915 Second Avenue
Seattle, WA 98174
(Kiosk Location)

WEST VIRGINIA
(Contact the Dayton, Ohio, center)

WISCONSIN
(Contact the Twin Cities, Minnesota, center)

WYOMING
(Contact the Denver, Colorado, center)

CHAPTER SEVEN

Patriotic Careers on Foreign Soil

"My country is the world, and my religion is to do good." THOMAS PAINE

Foreign Correspondents

*I*n an effort to stay abreast of all newsworthy events abroad, foreign correspondents are employed by networks, news services, television or radio stations, and major magazines or newspapers. They may also operate as freelance agents.

Acting as reporters, foreign correspondents are sent overseas to various countries where they are responsible for tracking down and uncovering information via news conferences, research, private sources, wire services, interviews and any other ways they can devise. They are then required to organize the information and produce articles that are clear, concise, and well written for their audiences in the United States or their "home" country. Since newsworthy events may occur at any time, being a foreign correspondent is hardly a nine-to-five job. And since many newsworthy events are also dangerous, this ingredient is also a part of the job.

Qualifications and Training

In general, employers seek candidates with a degree in journalism or broadcast communications or possibly a liberal arts degree with a strong background and experience in journalism. Skills in word processing, outstanding written and oral communication skills, a "nose for news," an ability to handle difficult situations, curiosity, research skills, persistence, patience, fortitude, honesty, and good "people skills" are some desirable qualities. You can expect serious competition for foreign correspondent positions— only reporters with extensive experience will be given the opportunity to function as foreign correspondents.

Those who are considering this kind of work should focus on classes in political science, world history, law, economics, psychology, foreign language, English, journalism, sociology, and communications. Practical experience through school newspapers, yearbooks, local newspapers, and internships in this or a related field are invaluable.

Salaries

Depending on the employer, the location, and the correspondent's previous experience, salaries can range from $20,000 to $75,000 or more.

Meet Jerry King, Foreign Correspondent

"Originally, my desire was to pursue a career in education," says Jerry King, a foreign correspondent for ABC-TV for more than fifteen years. "I was planning to teach physical education, an area I always enjoyed. So, I spent one year at the university in Canada but unfortunately didn't do well in chemistry and physics. Since these were both requirements for my major, I was afraid I might be taking those classes every year forever.

"Subsequently, I got into broadcasting and began doing sports, particularly hockey, in Canada. Then I moved to Bermuda, worked there for a summer doing a radio DJ show and news and television sports, and then moved to England and began working for United Press International in their radio/audio division from 1968 to 1971. That year, I switched over to ABC radio and worked there as a freelance radio journalist until 1975. That led to a television correspondence job in Germany. Late that year, I went to Beirut, where I worked for five and a half years before returning to the United States. Back in the United States, I received a call from some friends overseas saying they needed a correspondent. Was I interested in coming over? I conferred with my supervisors in New York, who were thrilled that I wanted to go back. So I went to Germany and got involved in all the upheaval in Berlin.

"As a foreign correspondent, you have to be able to function in a variety of circumstances," King stresses. "During my career, I've been assigned to Northern Ireland, Vietnam, Lebanon, Afghanistan, Somalia, Iran, Iraq—the list goes on and on. In these situations, you have to exist without the creature comforts of home and also be creative and quick thinking. I've been in Beirut cut off from all outside contact for weeks on end—without telephones or any other form of communication. When we filmed scenes, we sometimes shot them with two cameras, hoping that at least one roll of film would make it out of the country.

"Foreign correspondents must rely on local journalists—the people who live and work in the area. When I was living in Germany, for example, when Helmut Kohl wanted to say or do something, he didn't exactly call me up; his people called up the local reporters and got the word out through them. Maybe afterwards I could go back and get a particular slant or ask some specific questions, but my original information came from other journalists. The only exception is if you're on the spot of a breaking story, a hijacking for instance, where you can observe firsthand what is happening. I was lucky—in Poland I had a translator, a secretary, who knew Lech Walesa personally, so we had more access to him than some of the other journalists. I also had a cameraman in Lebanon who on Christmas day went around taking cookies to all the soldiers in the front lines because he wanted to make them his friends. He once told me that if you were caught some place with a group of 'bad people,' you should always shake hands and keep shaking hands because they don't like to shoot you when they're shaking hands.

"At one point, I was the first network television correspondent to come out of Warsaw after martial law was declared. We had been cut off so securely there from outside contact that the only thing we could hear was the BBC World Service shortwave broadcast. As time marched on, I thought the world had lost interest in the story, because the situation had not changed much. But when I was suddenly able to make my way out of the country by train, I was amazed at how much interest there actually was. ABC flew me to London quickly, arranged for me to board a Concord headed for New York, and the next day I appeared on the *David Brinkley Show*, *Good Morning America*, and *Sunday Morning*.

"I've seen humanity at its best and at its worst," King says. "As a foreign correspondent, you are allowed to meet some pretty interesting people and witness some really fascinating things. On the other hand, there's also a tremendous boredom factor sitting around in places like Baghdad where you're not allowed to do anything but wait. Getting through those days was not easy. And there are many times when you put in long hours researching, interviewing, writing, and rewriting your stories. Though being a foreign correspondent certainly involves hard work, it is incredibly enjoyable."

For Additional Information

Journalism Career and Scholarship Guide
Dow Jones Newspaper Fund
P.O. Box 300
Princeton, NJ 08543

Foreign Service Careers

Meet Geraldine Mosher, Foreign Service Careerist

Geraldine Mosher earned a B.A. from the University of Michigan at Ann Arbor with a major in English literature. She was employed from 1963 to 1983 by the Department of State in Washington, D.C.

"I was hired as a communications and records clerk," she says, "a position I landed by answering an advertisement in a post office and writing for information and an application. During my twenty-year career with the State Department, I was assigned to the following places: Washington, D.C.; Port-au-Prince, Haiti; Port of Spain, Trinidad; La Paz, Bolivia; Bonn, Germany; Belgrade, Yugoslavia; Recife, Brazil; Brasília, Brazil; Helsinki, Finland; Dakar, Senegal; and Guatemala City, Guatemala.

"My interest in doing this kind of work was sparked while at the University of Michigan, where I met and associated with many foreign students. I was interested in getting a job that allowed me to work overseas and to travel. I was inspired to work for the government because of President Kennedy.

"Also, my father was a World War I veteran and my mother was active in the American Legion Auxiliary, which provided me with one of the scholarships that I needed in order to go to college. I have always been very patriotic and, therefore, it was understandable that I would go to work for the government.

"Working in the communications field at a foreign service post is challenging and involves long hours and lots of dedication," she says. "It is, however, a vital job and gave me a feeling that what I was doing was important—that I was needed. My job involved all forms of communication and records—radio, telegraph, encryption, telephone, mail, diplomatic courier, filing, and so forth.

"At very large overseas posts (for example, Bonn, Germany), shift work was the rule. I would work two weeks on the day shift (8 A.M. to 4 P.M.), two weeks on the swing shift (4 P.M. to midnight) and two weeks on 'mids' (midnight to 8 A.M.). Socializing was not always easy because days off might be a Tuesday and Thursday or might be a Sunday and Monday, etc., so I was not off when others might be.

"At other posts, I would work days only (but that might be from 7 A.M. to 6 or 7 P.M.) and would also work half days on Saturday on a rotating basis. I also had to stand duty on a rotating basis (to be available for call-ins at any time of day or night). If the office had three communicators, duty was every third week; if there were only two, then duty was every other week. When on duty, you had to be in touch all the time. In many underdeveloped countries with unreliable phone service, I had to carry around a radio all the time. (Note: Modern technology has made radios and cell phones, etc., smaller, but, during my years of service, I used radios that were quite heavy.)

"Work was usually busy (sometimes hectic). In case of any emergencies (uprising, coup d'état, flood, VIP visits, and so on), the communicators all worked throughout until the emergency was over.

"Some places where I worked were very dangerous because of shootings, embassy bombings, and kidnappings. Others were very dangerous because of conditions that could severely affect health (such as malaria, plague, extremely high altitude, bad water).

"What I liked most about my career in the foreign service was one, the feeling that my job was vital and two, the social life (because of transfers, one was accepted and invited immediately upon arrival, and friendships were formed quickly). I also liked being able to travel, seeing different places, and getting to know (and hopefully understand) other cultures.

"What I liked least about the foreign service was the stress that I had to work under—stress caused by political upheavals and stress caused by close living and working conditions—not being able to really 'get away' from the job.

"I would advise anyone wanting to follow in my footsteps simply to go for it! Working with the foreign service is wonderful, challenging, and fulfilling. Working overseas is very educational and makes you realize how great our country really is."

Careers in Space

"Walking in space, man has never looked more puny or more significant." ALEXANDER CHASE

The space age began in the United States with the establishment of the National Aeronautics and Space Administration (NASA) in 1957. Created as a response to the launch of Sputnik I by the Soviet Union, the agency's first goal was realized in 1969 when Neil Armstrong landed on the moon. Space flights became almost routine until the near tragedy of Apollo 13 and the deaths of the astronauts aboard the Challenger spacecraft reminded all of us how dangerous space travel can be.

A host of people are needed in varying capacities in order to maintain the space program. At the center of the program are our heroes—the astronauts.

Though the word *astronaut* means "sailor among the stars," astronauts spend most of their time on the ground, preparing themselves to learn how to operate in space and gain knowledge of new horizons.

Once astronauts are chosen and assigned to missions, they take their places as part of space shuttle crews that consist of at least five people: the commander, the pilot, and three mission specialists, all of whom are NASA astronauts. Some flights also call for payload specialists. Sometimes, engineers, technicians, physicians, meteorologists, or biologists are also included. Crew members are trained and cross trained so that each one can handle at least one other associate's duties if necessary.

Pilots and commanders are both pilot astronauts who know how to fly aircraft and spacecraft. Commanders are in charge of the overall mission. They maneuver the orbiter, supervise the crew and the operations of the vehicle, and are responsible for the success and safety of the flight. Pilots help the commanders control and operate the orbiter and may help manipulate satellites by using a remote-control system. Like other crew members, they sometimes do work outside the craft or look after the payload.

While aboard, astronauts conduct experiments and other types of research under conditions of near-zero gravity. Laboratories may focus on or be related to earth sciences, astronomy, or manufacturing. Astronauts may also be in charge of deploying, servicing, or retrieving satellites or working with meters, sensors, special cameras, or other technical equipment. While in space, astronauts are able to increase our knowledge by observing the solar system and the Earth, for example, its geological formations or pollution currents.

Training reaches its peak a few weeks prior to the flight when fight crew and ground controllers go through the entire mission in a joint training exercise.

Qualifications and Training

At the high school level, it is important for would-be candidates to earn high marks and score well on standardized tests (SAT and/or ACT). The minimum degree requirement for candidates is a bachelor's degree from an accredited institution.

There are many degree options in the science departments at colleges and universities. Of interest is the fact that funds are contributed by NASA to fifty-one colleges and universities through its Space Grant Consortia. If you attend any of these schools, you are ensured that the curriculum for space programs offered will conform to the guidelines NASA has established. For lists of the schools write to NASA Education Division, Code FEO2, 300 E Street SW, Washington, DC 20546.

Astronauts come from both military and civilian backgrounds. Pilots are chosen exclusively from a pool of high-achieving jet pilots who have accumulated more than one thousand hours of time in the air. Most pilot/commanders are individuals who have served or are currently serving in the armed forces. Civilian mission specialists are those with advanced training in areas such as astronomy, biology, medicine, or mathematics.

The Astronaut Selection Board (ASB) seeks those who have a strong technical background and highly regarded recommendations from undergraduate and graduate school professors who can attest to problem-solving abilities, communicability with others, and ability to work well as part of a team. Those who have all the qualifications may send in U.S. Government Application Form 171 to the Johnson Space Center in Houston, Texas.

The ASB interviews each person and assigns them a rating based on experience, expertise (physicists, chemists, biologists, etc.), potential, motivations, ability to function as a member of a team, communicative abilities, and adaptability. Based on ASB recommendations, the NASA administrator makes the final selection for a rigorous training program.

Similar to other applications processes, aspiring astronauts compete with a formidable number of candidates—in this case, an average of 4,014 candidates for about twenty slots that open up every two years.

During training at the Johnson Space Center in Houston, Texas, astronauts must take further course work in areas such as astronomy, meteorology, and computers. They also spend time in weightless simulation drills learning how to conduct necessary work while wearing a space suit.

Job Settings

Since recruitment for astronauts is ongoing, applications can be mailed at any time. Apply to Astronaut Selection Board, AH611, Johnson Space Center, Houston, TX 77058.

Pilot and mission astronauts work mainly at the Lyndon B. Johnson Space Center in Houston, Texas. Other NASA space centers include Ames Research Center, Moffett Field, California; Goddard Space Flight Center, Greenbelt, Maryland; George C. Marshall Space Flight Center, Huntsville, Alabama; John F. Kennedy Space Center, Florida; Langley Research Center, Hampton, Virginia; Lewis Research Center, Cleveland, Ohio; Stennis Space Center, Bay Saint Louis, Mississippi.

Salaries for Astronauts

Astronauts begin their salaries in accordance with the U.S. government pay scale at GS-11 or 12 (approximately $45,000 to $50,000) status and may elevate to a GS-15 rating (approximately $68,000 to $90,000).

Meet James Arthur Lovell Jr., Astronaut

As a high school junior, James Arthur Lovell Jr., with the help of a chemistry teacher and two friends, launched a rocket. Though it rose only eighty feet in the air and was only partially successful,

Lovell knew even then that he longed for a career in rocket science. True to his ambition, Lovell became a navy test pilot and was chosen to be an astronaut in 1962. He served as module pilot for the Apollo 8 mission (the first manned flight to orbit the moon), as a member of the Gemini 7 crew (in space for two weeks), worked with pilot Edwin Aldrin on Gemini 12, and served as commander of Apollo 13 in 1970. The Apollo 13 mission was very nearly a disaster when an explosion caused the shuttle to lose oxygen and power. For four days, the world waited and prayed that somehow the astronauts would make it back home safely.

The story of the Apollo 13 mission was made into a movie (based upon Lovell's book, originally titled *Lost Moon*), a box-office success, with actor Tom Hanks playing the part of Lovell. To become familiar with the details, Hanks traveled to meet and fly with Lovell a year earlier. "I tried to convey my feelings, actions, views, goals, and inner being to him, so he could gain some insights and a perception of the character," explains Lovell.

"I loved my career so much that, to tell you the truth, I would have worked for NASA for nothing," says Lovell. "It was such an amazing and interesting job. And I wasn't the only one who felt this way. So did most of the other astronauts and a lot of other people who worked for NASA. The attrition rate at the time was almost zero because no one wanted to leave. That's because the sense of achievement and satisfaction you receive as an astronaut for a job well done is incredible—pioneering new avenues, new vistas, seeing things for the first time. Apollo 8 was an awe-inspiring flight because my mission mates and I were the first to see the far side of the moon. So it's obviously one of the great milestones of my career.

"I feel that, in order to become a successful astronaut, a candidate must have the following qualities: curiosity, the ability to handle stress, the facility to work well in team situations, the initiative to see problems and overcome them, sufficient training in a particular discipline such as biology or engineering, and the ability to perform optimally with only five or six hours of sleep per night! It's also important to be goal oriented and persistent. You need to be the kind of person who is motivated to stretch to accomplish goals and be qualified and ready to enhance luck to make it work for you in the best way possible.

"No matter what, I feel NASA will continue its efforts because it has proven to be a viable, creative program. Funding will fluctuate up and down and the numbers of people involved may vary, but it will always attract well-qualified individuals who are motivated to explore new worlds and share in the thrill of learning things we never knew before."

For Additional Information

Check out NASA on the Internet at http://www.nasa.gov/.

About the Author

J an Goldberg's love for the printed page began well before her second birthday. Regular visits to the book bindery where her grandfather worked produced a magic combination of sights and smells that she carries with her to this day.

Childhood was filled with composing poems and stories, reading books, and playing library. Elementary and high school included an assortment of contributions to school newspapers. While a full-time college student, Goldberg wrote extensively as part of her job responsibilities in the College of Business Administration at Roosevelt University in Chicago. After receiving a degree in elementary education, she was able to extend her love of reading and writing to her students.

Goldberg has written extensively in the occupations area for General Learning Corporation's *Career World Magazine*, as well as for the many career publications produced by CASS Communications. She has also contributed to a number of projects for educational publishers, including Free Spirit Publishing, Capstone Publishing, Publications International, Scott Foresman, Addison-Wesley, and Camp Fire Boys and Girls.

As a feature writer, Goldberg's work has appeared in *Parenting Magazine, Today's Chicago Woman, Opportunity Magazine, Chicago Parent, Correspondent, Opportunity Magazine, Successful Student, Complete Woman, North Shore Magazine*, and the *Pioneer Press* newspapers. In all, she has published more than three hundred pieces as a full-time freelance writer.

In addition to *Careers for Patriotic Types and Others Who Want to Serve Their Country*, she is the author of fifteen other career books published by NTC/Contemporary Publishing Group, Inc.